BADMINTON TO THE TOP

BADMINTON TO THE TOP

DEREK TALBOT

EP PUBLISHING LIMITED

First published 1981 by EP Publishing Limited,
East Ardsley, Wakefield, West Yorkshire, England.

ISBN: 0 7158 0641 6

First edition 1981

Acknowledgements

Photographs by Louis Ross
Design and artwork by Caroline Reeves

Typeset by CTL Computer Typesetters Ltd., Leeds
Printed in Great Britain by MacLehose Ltd., Glasgow

CONTENTS

CHAPTER 1
THE AUTHOR ·

Derek Talbot and Gillian Gilks upon winning the All-England mixed doubles.

Derek Talbot, now thirty-four years of age, has been England's leading male badminton player for more than ten years. His career in badminton has taken him to all four corners of the earth, and he can boast an impressive string of victories almost too numerous to list. Suffice it to say that with more than eighty appearances for England to his credit, his achievements include ten national titles, twenty International titles, three European Games gold medals and four Commonwealth Games gold medals. He is one of the very few world class badminton all-rounders, equally at home on the singles or the doubles court, and hence well equipped to help others in any department of the game.

Born in Newcastle-upon-Tyne, he was still in nappies when introduced to the game by his parents Gwen and Eddie, who played in the First Division of the Northern Counties League. By the age of twelve he had developed quite an interest in the sport, but it was unheard of for one so young to join a club. Derek had to content himself with watching his parents play, and paradoxically he owes much of his success to this fact. He plagued his father with so many questions about the game during this watching period that he became a useful tactician long before he had played his first complete match of badminton.

At thirteen, while a student at Heaton Grammar School, he was allowed to join his first club, and at fourteen he joined his first senior club. With his head full of ideas on the game progress was rapid, and at sixteen years of age he was representing Northumberland. Further progress was made whilst he was at University, for he not only captained the University team but also represented British Universities in several of their fixtures against International sides. When he graduated, his ambition to play for England took top priority and he decided to move to London, recognised at that time as the centre of the sport. After only a few months in the big city he had established himself as one of the best players in the country and was selected to represent England on a tour of South Africa with the legendary Tony Jordan MBE as captain.

This was to be the start of a long and successful playing career during which he experienced play in the true-blue amateur days, through the sham-amateur days, and in the modern days of open badminton.

An insatiable appetite for the game, a great tactical brain and an unquestionable desire to win are the qualities which have helped Derek Talbot make his mark in English badminton.

CHAPTER 2
INTRODUCTION

It is the purpose of this book to impart the knowledge and experience which I have gained over the past ten years, one of the most important decades in the history of badminton.

The name of the game ten years ago was fun. The life-style of an international badminton player could quite easily include parties, hangovers, girls, the lot – and it very often did. Many players were known to have a brandy before a top match and some were known to have several.

I can recall a final of the West German Championships when Elliot Stuart and I were up against the Malaysian pair of Ng Boon Bee and Punch Gunalan. The preliminaries to this match were quite interesting, for Elliot and I were legless after consuming preposterous quantities of German schnapps, while the Malaysian pair had been forced to spend the night in a telephone kiosk after going out on the town and finding it impossible to get into their hotel. I am afraid to confess that not even the effect of an ice-cold shower prior to the match was sufficient to counter the effect of the schnapps and the telephone kiosk boys won. However, I hasten to add that in a more serious encounter at the All-England Championships some few weeks later, Elliot and I gained our revenge.

In recent years the game has taken on a different aspect because of the introduction of something new – money. There is now financial importance in being a winner and consequently changes in playing styles have evolved, with a very strong accent on physical preparation. Life at the top is possibly less exciting these days, for sadly many of the pleasures in life have an adverse effect on one's stamina, but the compensations which make everything worthwhile are the financial reward and the feeling of success. Of course there are still some 'Nastases' in the badminton world, but they are becoming fewer.

Many people say from time to time, 'I wonder how old champions like Dave Freeman would fare today?' Well, I believe that if they played as they did in their day, they would not be in the same league as today's champions. However, if they had learned their badminton in today's climate then I am sure it would be a different story, for they were people of undoubted talent. Of course, the game was much slower then. One only has to see a film of Fred Perry in his heyday and compare the play with that of a modern-day tennis champion such as Bjorn Borg to realise how games change with time, and badminton is no exception. Many people believe that developments in badminton have resulted in a loss of flair. However, we still have our players of natural talent but they have to use their flair in a tougher, faster, more effective style of game.

As a founder member and present Chairman of the B.P.A. (Badminton Players' Association), I have been closely involved in the developments which have led to what we now know as Open Badminton. I am quite sure that we are to see even greater changes in future years, for with the game booming in so many countries it is now big business. The television companies are allocating more and more time to badminton, and because of this sponsors are becoming more and more interested in our game. The appeal is world-wide, with eastern and western countries alike good at the sport.

I see the USA as the country with a lot to offer in coming years. They have had their champions in the past but in latter years have been relatively uninterested in world events. But Americans are not likely to give up the chance of an involvement in a big business, and that is what badminton is today. So let us hope that some of the thousands of dollars currently being injected into other sports will come the way of badminton and help it become one of the greatest international sports of all time.

The earnings of most of the world's top players are not known by the younger players who are striving for the top. This is not a good thing. In England a young boy will have a good idea of what a professional footballer might earn and certainly he will be able to fit the footballer into a particular income bracket. This gives the young boy the incentive to try and make it to the top himself.

As badminton grows in importance and is more publicised, the earnings of those at the top will become known to the up-and-comings and there will be the incentive for many who would otherwise have chosen another sport as their career to concentrate on badminton. So let me say that, at present, several players earn more than £20,000 per annum and this figure is likely to have increased substantially by the time this book is printed. I hope this will give some of our better athletes the incentive to give badminton a real try, for I am sure it has much to offer.

Every top player has his own formulae for success, but there are several basic ingredients common to all. It is the aim of this book to familiarise you with these ingredients. With this knowledge you should have the basis to lift your game to county level, international level and further. Most people have the talent to be international sportsmen of one kind or another, but unfortunately they do not know how to bring these talents out in themselves. So, as you read this book, learn as much as possible but above all believe in yourself, for with this belief and a great deal of effort real success is possible.

CHAPTER 3
BASIC STROKES

The Clear

The point of impact is directly above the head. To maximise power the arm is straightened at the moment the shuttle is struck. Rotation of the forearm is also a vital movement in the production of power. Many top players can play powerful strokes with a bent arm action because they are utilising a strong turning movement of forearm and wrist.

Note the position of readiness, with the racket held at the side of the head. From this position, moving the body back from the waist, swing forwards through the point of impact. This demonstrates the short swing, which is most commonly used today. Some players prefer a long swing whereby they move their racket in a downwards direction after the position of readiness and then round in a large arc. This loopy swing is

Forehand Clear

Position of Readiness.

Body bending back just before impact.

Impact directly above the head.

Short swing follow through.

Backhand Clear

Preparing for the stroke.

Elbow leading stroke – wrist cocked with racket at right angles to forearm.

Turning action of forearm and wrist prior to impact.

Short turning action now complete.

fine if you have sufficient time to play your stroke. However, on many occasions you haven't, and therefore the short swing is to be preferred.

The action of the clear is very much a throwing action and you can understand the stroke better if you picture yourself throwing a stone. The action is produced by a system of levers made up of the three joints of the arm, the shoulder, elbow and wrist. These joints straighten in sequence just before impact and, together with the turning action of elbow and wrist, produce the power. Bending of the torso at the hips is also important in producing power, as this adds body weight to the stroke. The same principles apply for the backhand clear, but the wrist turns in the opposite direction. Consider the arm action in the photographs shown above.

Most top players cock their wrists to help produce the best turning action. This prevents the player from holding the racket in a straight line with his arm, which normally produces a very weak shot.

The Smash

The point of impact is slightly in front of that found in a clear. The wrist action propels the shuttlecock in the desired downwards direction. The same short action is used for the smash as for the clear.

To get extra power many players jump off the ground. They do so as the shuttlecock is approaching the target area so that their body is on its way down at the moment of impact; thus

Forehand Smash

Position of Readiness.

Jumping showing the body bending backwards and the scissor leg action.

Body starting to move down. Bodyweight moving forward from hips, shuttle struck in front of head.

Turning action of forearm and wrist now complete. Feet touching floor to regain balance.

Short follow through back to a position of readiness.

Preparing for the stroke.

Cocked wrist. Forearm starting to rotate.

Forearm straightens and wrist follows through to direct shuttle downwards.

Short follow through.

the weight of the body is translated into racket energy, thereby increasing the power of the shot. Jumping is uncommon with the backhand smash, and in fact should be avoided. The extra power here is provided by the turning action of the body at the hips, which is most easily produced when the feet are firmly placed on the ground together with the turning action of the forearm and wrist. The photographs above show the backhand smash.

The Drop

The action is the same as the clear but with a gentle locking of the wrist just before impact. With such an action it is difficult

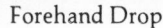

Forehand Drop

Position of readiness.

Impact directly above head.

Just after impact wrist following through to direct shuttle gently downwards.

Short follow through back to a position of readiness.

for your opponent to detect whether your shot is to be a clear or a drop.

The Service

The position of the feet is important with the service as they govern the direction of the follow-through of the racket. For a right-handed player the left foot should be slightly in front of the right foot with feet a short distance apart. The shuttlecock can be held in a number of different ways, but if possible holding the glued portion of the shuttlecock should be avoided.

The wrist should be cocked so as to allow for a well-

15

Preparing for the stroke. Feet a short distance apart.

Wrist cocked. Racket hand moving forward. Eye on the net tape.

Shuttle dropped onto racket. Wrist remains cocked to ensure low trajectory. Eyes moving from net to shuttle.

Short arm action with wrist remaining cocked. Eyes move from shuttle to target area.

Short follow through. Eyes now on shuttle as it approaches opponent.

disguised flick service. The arm action is a gentle push, ensuring that you have your eyes on the shuttle at the moment of impact. It is a good idea to look at the level of the net while you are preparing for this stroke. This gives you an impression of the correct height of your intended trajectory, and your mind can store this information even when your eyes are on the shuttle at the moment of impact.

The Drive

The racket is held so as to form an extension of the arm. As I have mentioned when discussing the clear, this weaker wrist action does not normally produce maximum power, and it is for this reason that a strong arm action is required for the drive. A low trajectory close to net height is needed. The drive can be

Preparing for the stroke.

Elbow moving forward. Wrist and racket lag behind.

Racket moving forward to the point of impact.

Follow through of strong arm action.

particularly effective in doubles play but can also be effective in singles as a surprise shot if used sparingly.

It is quite common for the thumb to be placed up the handle of the racket so as to achieve maximum directional control. This grip position is most effective when the shuttle is struck slightly in front of the body.

The Underarm Clear

A common return of a drop shot or a net shot is a high underarm clear to the back of the court. The shuttle is struck as close to the top of the net as possible. It is important to develop a short sharp follow-through otherwise you will be quite likely to hit the net with your racket, which of course is a fault.

Forearm Underarm Clear

Lunge movement bringing racket
into target area – wrist cocked.

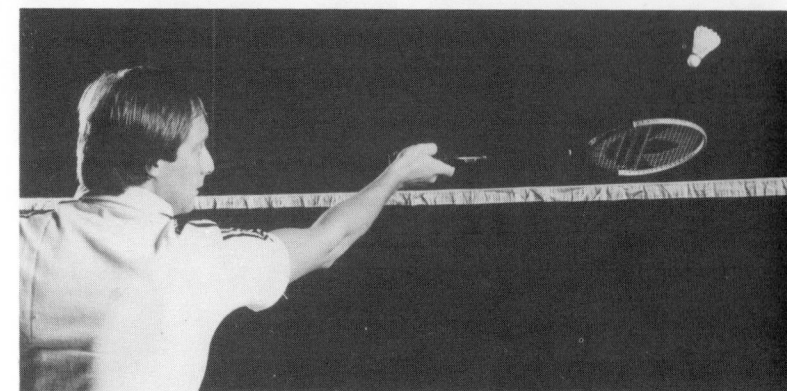

Taking the shuttle at tape height just
as it crosses the net.

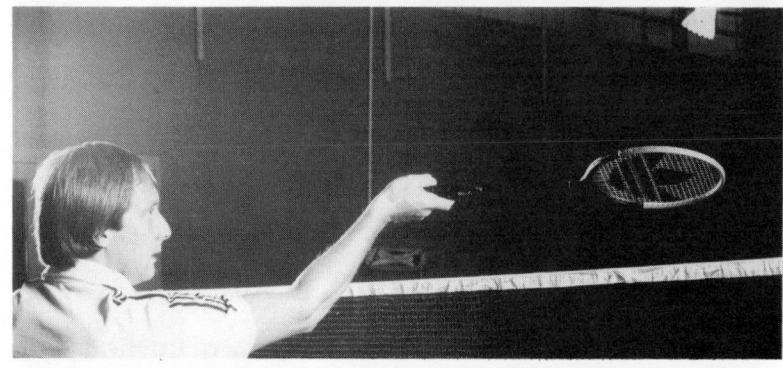

Turning action of forearm and wrist
pushing shuttle high into the air.

Short sharp follow through. Balance
is still good.

Position of readiness. Racket out in front. Backhand grip.

Arm moves forward. Wrist is cocked and locked on impact.

Arm moves forward after stroke. Wrist remains cocked.

Short follow through. Balance is good.

The Block Return

Generally the easiest way to win a point is to hit the shuttle in a downwards direction. It is important, therefore, to get your opponent to lift the shuttlecock whenever possible. One way of doing so is by turning your opponent's attack into defence using block defence. The secret is to remain relaxed no matter how hard the smash you are trying to return. Try to take the shuttle out in front of you. A very gentle stroke is all that is required.

CHAPTER 4
ADVANCED STROKE TECHNIQUES

I am assuming that the reader is already accomplished in the basic strokes such as clear, drop, smash, drive and low and high service. If so, there are certain advanced strokes you should know about which form a very important part of the repertoire of a top-class player. The execution and implications of these strokes are not normally fully understood by the average club or even county player.

Racket Grip
Before going into the details of the advanced strokes, I would first like to mention racket grip. While every player has a

Racket Grip

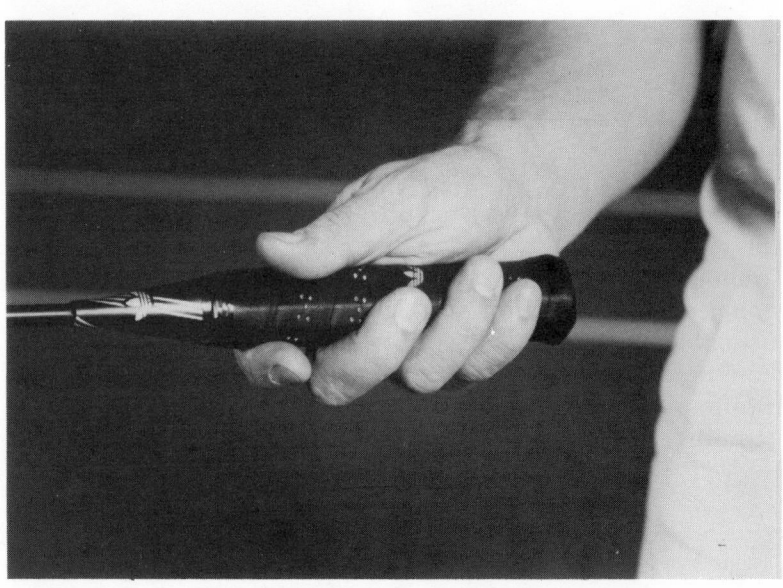

Correct grip with fingers spread along racket handle.

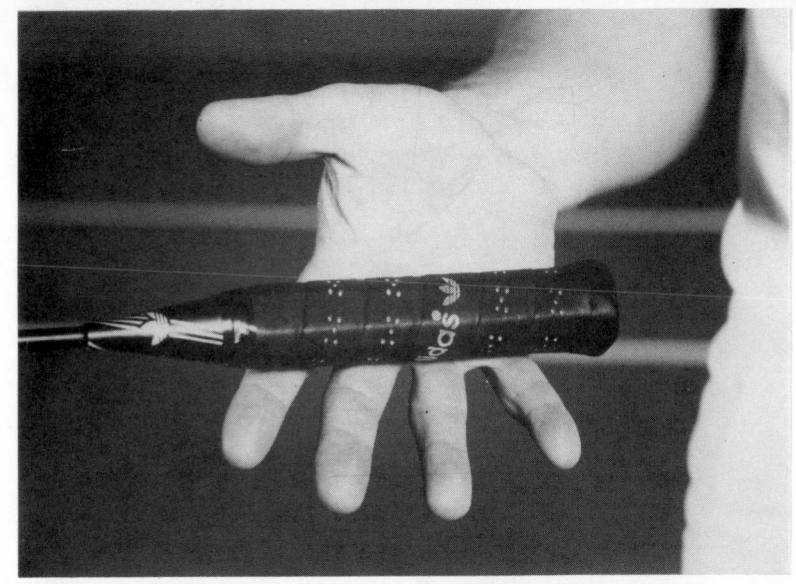

Correct – racket handle across base of fingers.

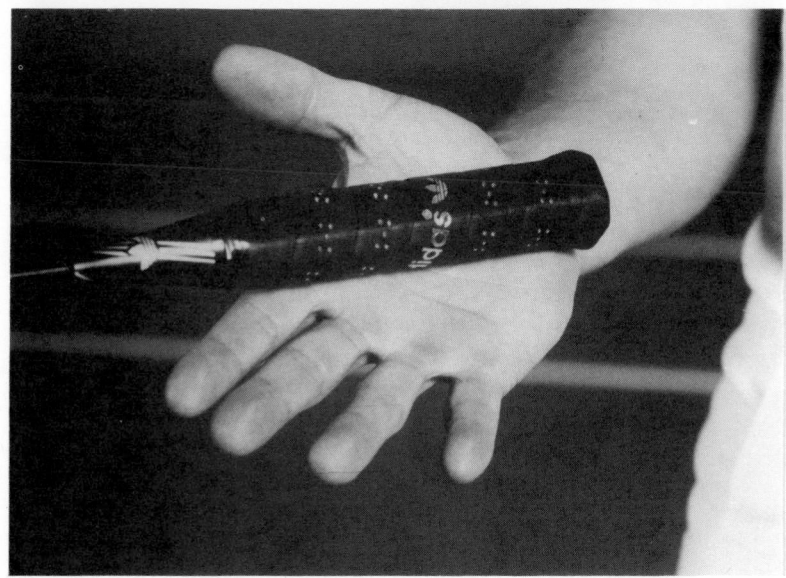

Wrong – racket handle across palm of hand.

slightly different way of holding his racket it is impossible to play the full range of strokes using the same grip, and consequently most top players change their grip several times during the course of a rally. Because the game demands very fast reflexes it is obvious that one must be able to change grip quickly. This is achieved by turning the racket in the hand with the fingers. In order for this to be done the handle must be held across the base of the fingers and not across the palm of the hand. This is a common fault and well worthy of note. The photographs above illustrate the point.

The Slice Drop

The first advanced stroke we shall look at is the sliced drop. This stroke is performed by slicing or brushing the shuttle rather than patting it. In the forehand drop the grip used is as below. This grip is commonly known as the chopping-axe grip for obvious reasons.

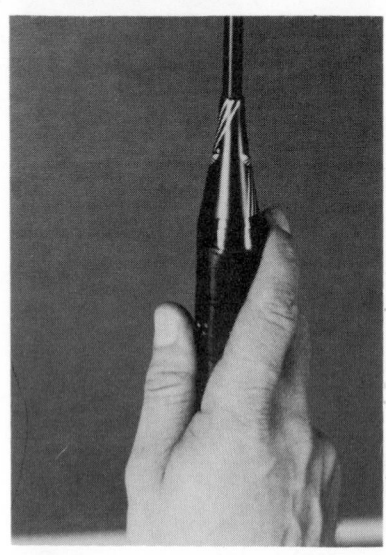

Chopping Axe Grip

Below we see the actual stroke, with the head of the racket travelling at an angle of approximately forty-five degrees to the intended direction of the shuttle. This is the reason why this stroke is so deceptive, for the shuttle travels in a different direction to that of the racket and most players anticipate shots by watching the target area, i.e. the racket.

Forehand Straight Slice

Position of readiness.

Racket brushing shuttle which travels straight down the side line. Wrist and forearm rotate in a clockwise direction.

Racket following through diagonally across court 45° to direction of shuttle.

Short follow-through to position of readiness.

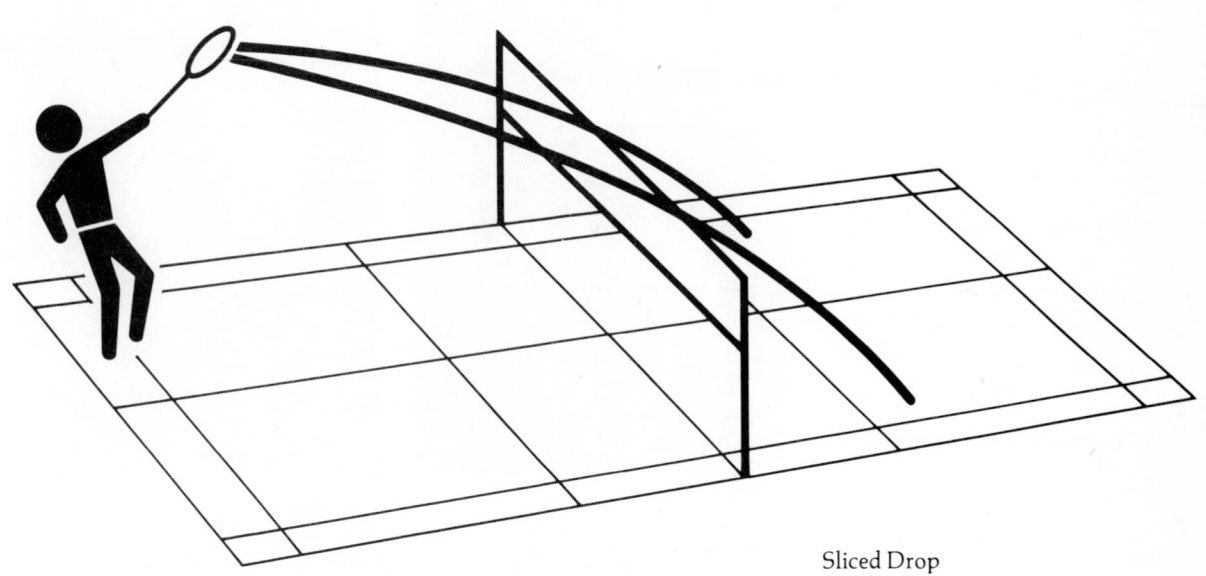

Sliced Drop

For a right-handed player the diagram above shows the area of the court penetrated by the two main forehand strokes.

A reverse slice can also be used but this is more difficult to perform as the wrist is required to turn the racket in a direction against the natural follow-through of the arm.

Position of body and racket just before stroke.

Transference of weight onto left leg.

Wrist and arm move forward after impact approx. 45° to direction of shuttle. Racket pointing out of court. Wrist and forearm rotate in an anticlockwise direction.

Short follow-through. Weight back on two feet. Balance good.

A very supple wrist is required for this stroke and the best results are often achieved using the frying-pan grip, shown opposite.

Once this stroke is mastered it can be extremely effective.

The same slice or brushing action can be applied to backhand drops, and very few players are more capable in this department of the game than Flemming Delfs, the former world champion.

On the next page we see Flemming playing one of his favourite shots, the cross-court backhand sliced drop. Exactly the same principles apply as for the forehand drop, but one

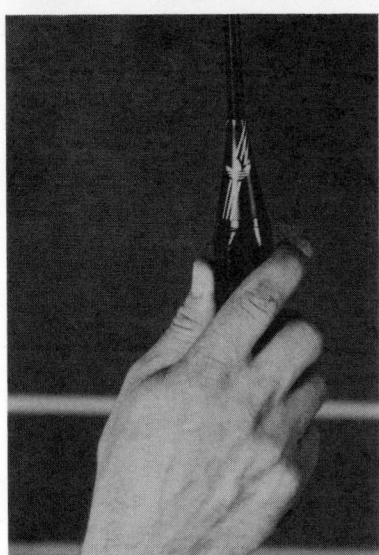

Frying Pan Grip

interesting point you will notice from the photograph is that the wrist is cocked and the racket is held at an angle of approximately ninety degrees to the forearm.

Flemming Delfs (Denmark)

The Sliced Smash and the Flat Smash

The smash is commonly used to finish off a rally, but variation of the smash is important. In a singles game a player will command the game from a small area in the centre of the court, known as his base. By occupying this base as often as possible one minimises the movement required to reach shots placed to all four corners of the court. It is therefore important to try and move your opponent from his natural base position. Movement from base simply opens up the court, making it easier to produce the winning shot. For example, several flat smashes will tend to move the base of your opponent back in the court, opening up the front area of the court. Alternatively, heavily sliced smashes will force him to the forecourt area, leaving the area at the back of the court vulnerable to an attacking clear. Different players have different natural bases according to their individual styles of play, stature etc., but they are all subject to pressure when forced to play from an unnatural base position.

Now that you understand the reasons for playing these strokes, we can consider the technique involved in their production. It is the wrist which dictates, just before the moment of impact, whether the smash is to be flat or sliced.

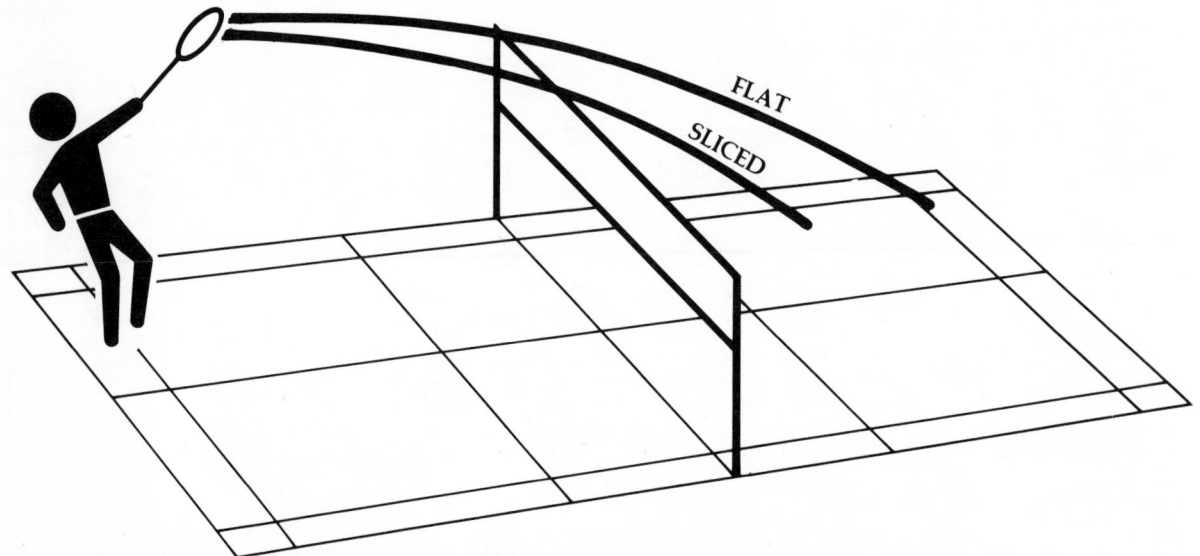

For those of us who do not have great wrist flexibility, a useful tip is to hold the racket with the 'chopping-axe' grip for the slice and the 'frying-pan' grip for the flat smash.

Apart from the aim of moving your opponent from his base you should also bear in mind that most people normally find it easier to defend certain types of smash. It is therefore necessary to experiment so that you can favour the type of smash your opponent least likes to receive. Another useful tip is to vary the pace of the smash, for many players with good reflexes are bemused by a smash which is travelling slower than anticipated.

One of the best exponents of the flat smash is Sture Johnsson of Sweden. The photograph below shows his use of a jumping action to produce extra power.

Sture Johnsson

The Attacking Clear/High Clear

Variation of the clear is again important in moving the base position of your opponent, particularly in singles. Both types of clear are intended to force your opponent to the back of the court, but good anticipation of the attacking clear can result in an early interception. Unless attacking clears are getting good results they should be used sparingly, otherwise your opponent will be able to play a large part of his game from an effectively shortened court. The most common difference between a good singles player and a bad one is his length of clear. Attacking clears are particularly effective against players who have a

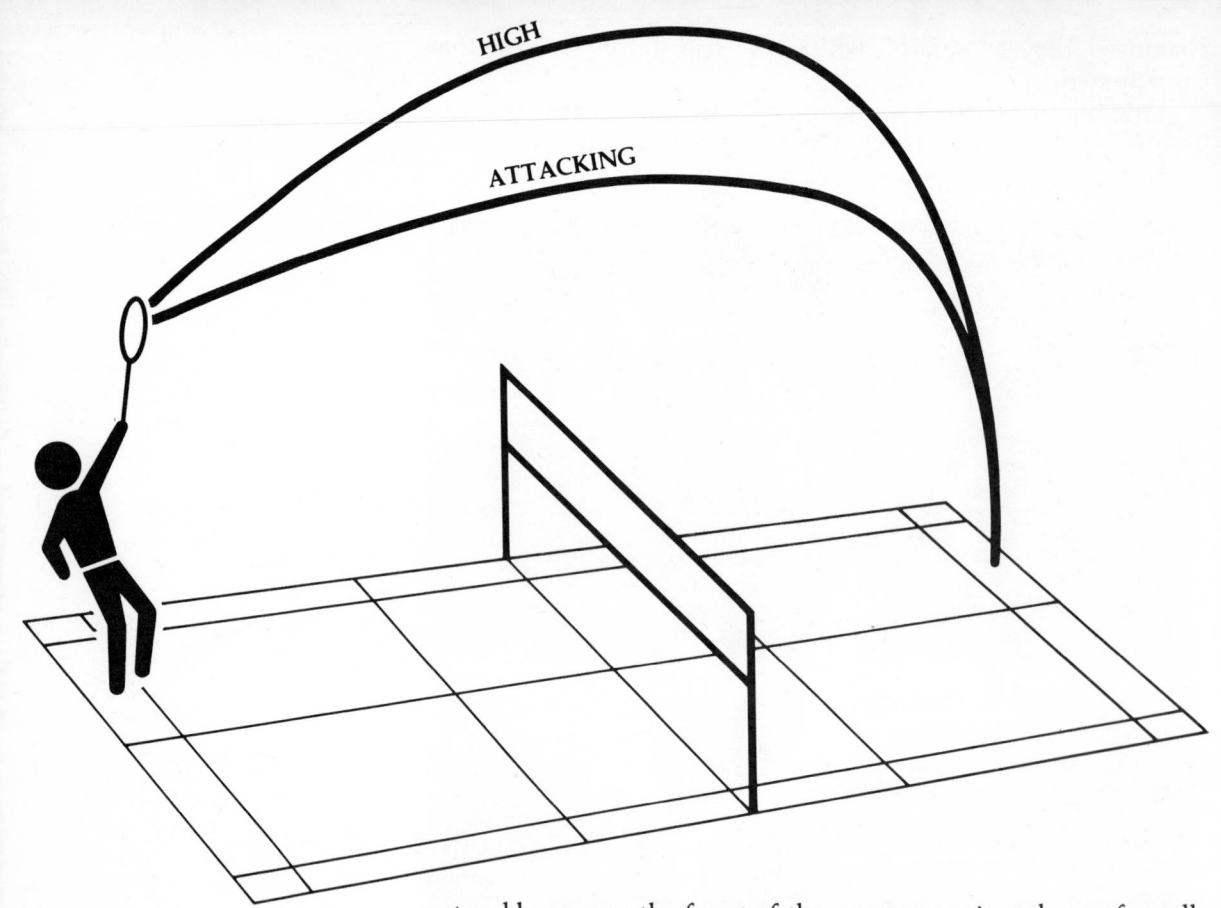

natural base near the front of the court or against those of small stature. However, they must be projected just above the reach of your opponent, forcing him to play them from the back of the court at a low height from the ground.

The Spin Net Shot and Tap Return
When the shuttle spins and tumbles close to the net it is extremely difficult to return. There are very few players who master the art of producing or returning this shot properly. Most players learn to 'chop' the shuttle so that it tumbles cork over feathers, but it is when this tumble is combined with a spin that it becomes most effective. The action of the racket is particularly important.

Note that the path of the racket is curved. In general, the best shots are produced when the shuttle is directed to a part of the court which allows its original direction to be maintained.

Practice routines can be very useful in mastering this shot. One player can practise a cross-court low service, allowing the other player to practise the net shot.

The return of this shot can be directed to the back of the court as an underarm clear or to the front of the court as a net shot or tap return.

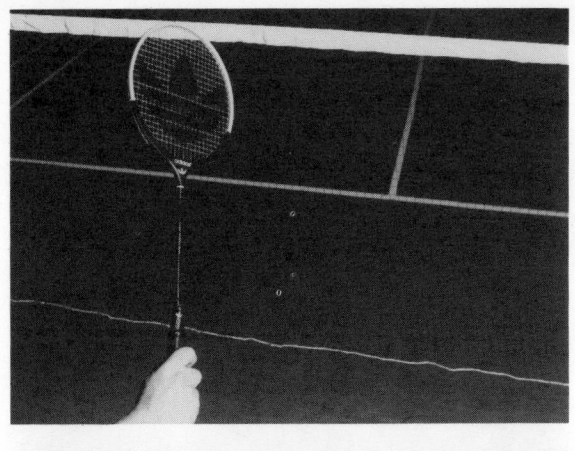

Forearm and wrist rotate in an anticlockwise direction. The racket follows a curved path. The shuttle is spun by making contact with both cork and feathers.

With the clear return the racket follows a curved path, slicing the shuttle, and a strong follow-through allows the shuttle to travel high to the back of the court.

In playing a net return it is important to strike the shuttle as close to the top of the net as possible. By stroking the shuttle with a curved action, as previously described, it is possible to

Backhand Sliced Underarm Clear

Lunge forward to position of readiness.

Wrist cocked. Racket head following curved path.

Racket strings stroking feathers and cork on impact.

Rotation of forearm and wrist complete.

Follow through.

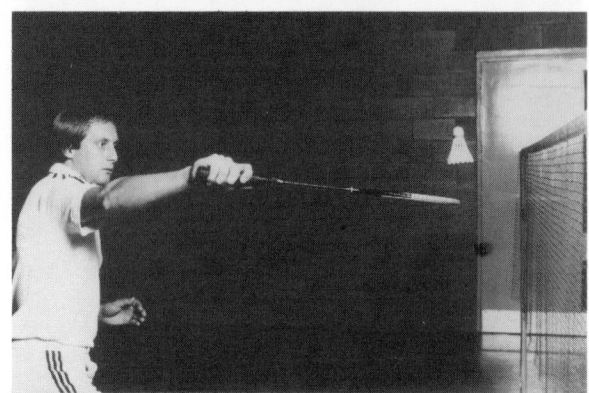

retain the spin on it. If the shuttle is played into the tape of the net, it is not uncommon for this spin to cause it to climb the tape and roll over the net onto the opponent's side.

The brush or tap return is the better shot to play as it puts more pressure on your opponent; if he sees that you intend to attack every loose net shot, he is quite likely to make errors. This shot must be played from above net height, and needs a short, sharp action of the wrist. If the shuttle is very near to net height the player will often brush or slice it so as to help prevent him hitting it into the net.

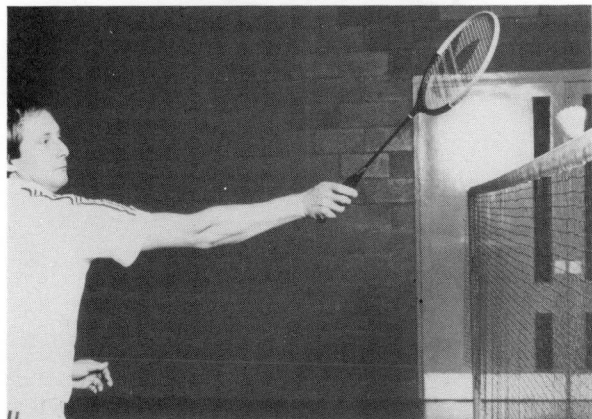
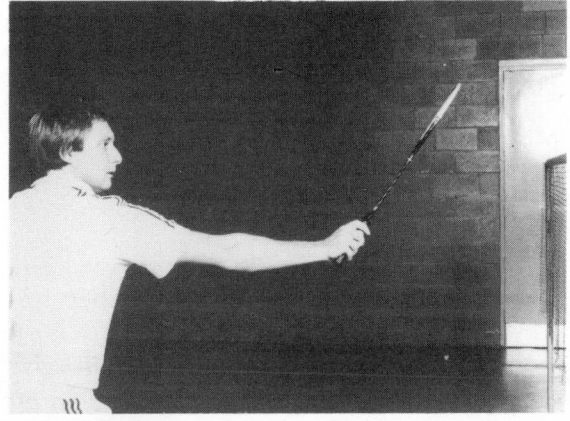

Forehand Brush Return

Lunge moving racket into target area.

Racket moves along the net from right to left.

Brushing the shuttle on impact.

Follow through.

Former European and All-England Champions.

Thomas Kihlström and Bengt Fröman, Sweden

Thomas Kihlström is a fine exponent of the brush return.

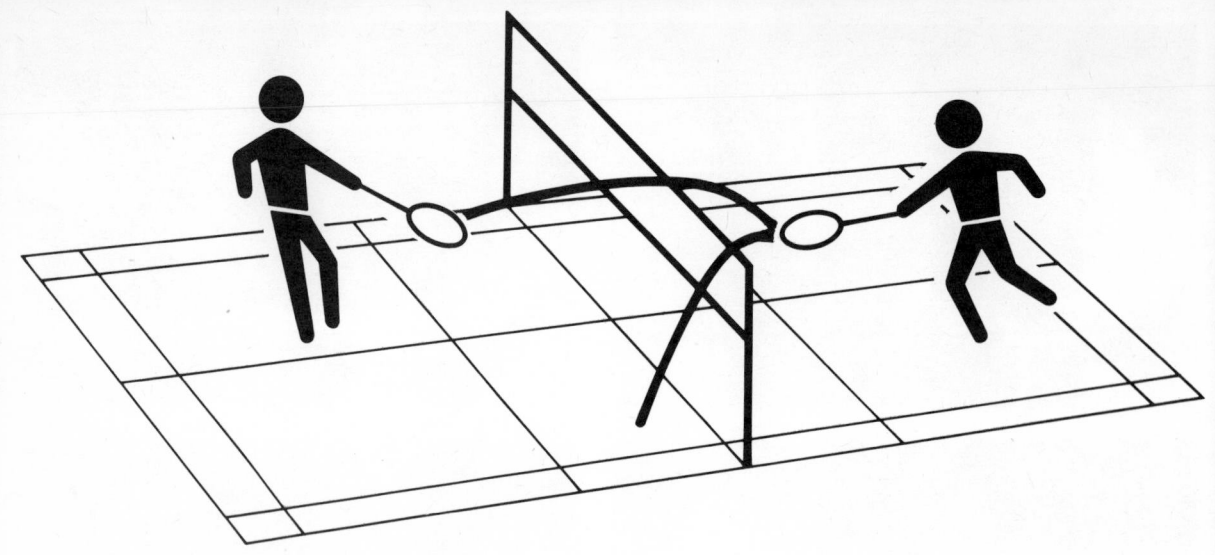

Low Service and receipt of Service

The Service and receipt of Service

Service is one department of the game where there are very few set rules. Most top players develop their own techniques, and these are so numerous it would be impossible to list even a small percentage in this book. However, there are certain golden rules and tips which I would like you to know about.

The following photographs show the backhand low service. It is particularly important to keep your eye on the shuttle at the moment of impact.

The backhand service has become very popular in recent years, for it has certain advantages over the forehand service in doubles. One advantage is that it gives the opponent the least possible time to anticipate the service, as the shuttle is normally struck closer to the net and with a much shorter arm action. Also, because the backhand action is normally a very short swing it is particularly hard to detect a flick service. By holding the shuttlecock upside down it is possible to brush the feathers, thus putting a strong spin on the shuttle and causing it to turn base over feathers.

However, it is the ability to vary your service, whether it be short, flick or high, which makes the difference between an ordinary service and a good one.

Low Service

Vary the position at which the shuttle crosses the net. It is quite common to find that a particular opponent is more effective in his return of the low service if the shuttle is directed to a certain

Backhand Low Service

Shuttle held upside down just above racket face. Strings slice feathers of shuttle causing it to spin and turn cork over feathers.

Racket follows anti clockwise curve on follow through.

area of the court. For example, it may be that he prefers a service directed to his forehand wing or alternatively one straight in front of him, or perhaps one directed to the centre of the court. If someone is continually attacking your service vary the position at which the shuttle crosses the net. If this is not successful then you can try the flick or high service as alternatives. I cannot stress enough the obvious – if you do not get the shuttle effectively into play you cannot win a point.

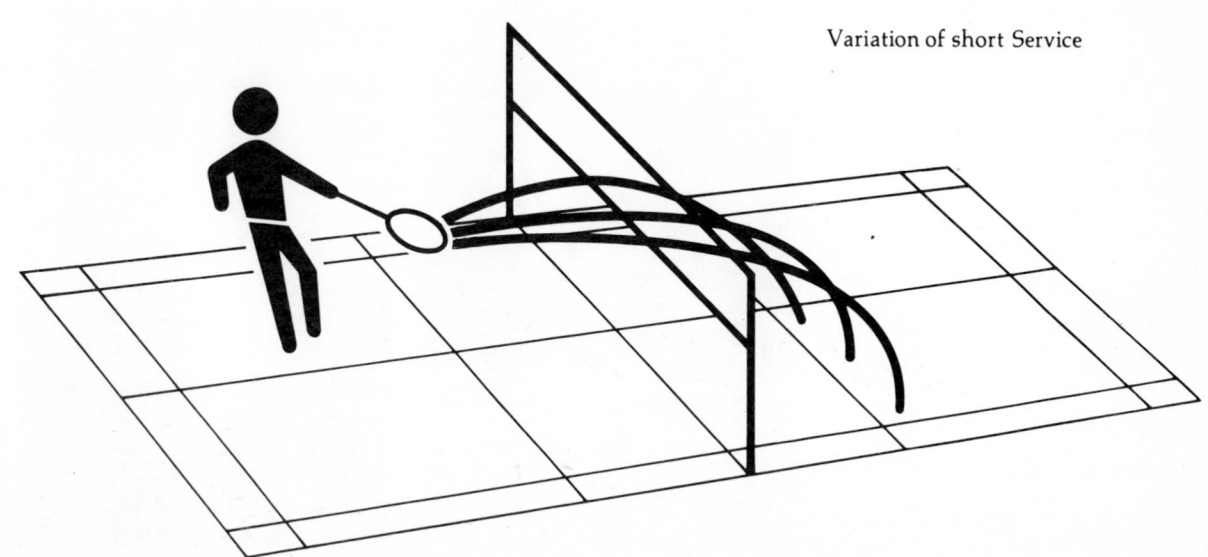

Variation of short Service

High Service

The high service is particularly useful in singles play, but it is important to ensure that you are using the full length of the court. As a check, look to see where your opponent's feet are just before the moment of impact. If they are not on or just behind the doubles service line then you are hitting short. Be careful not to strike the shuttle above the waist as this is a common fault and will be picked up by a service judge should you play in competition.

High Service

Position of readiness.

Wrist cocked. Eye on shuttle.

Shuttle struck below waist.

Follow through in intended direction of flight of shuttle.

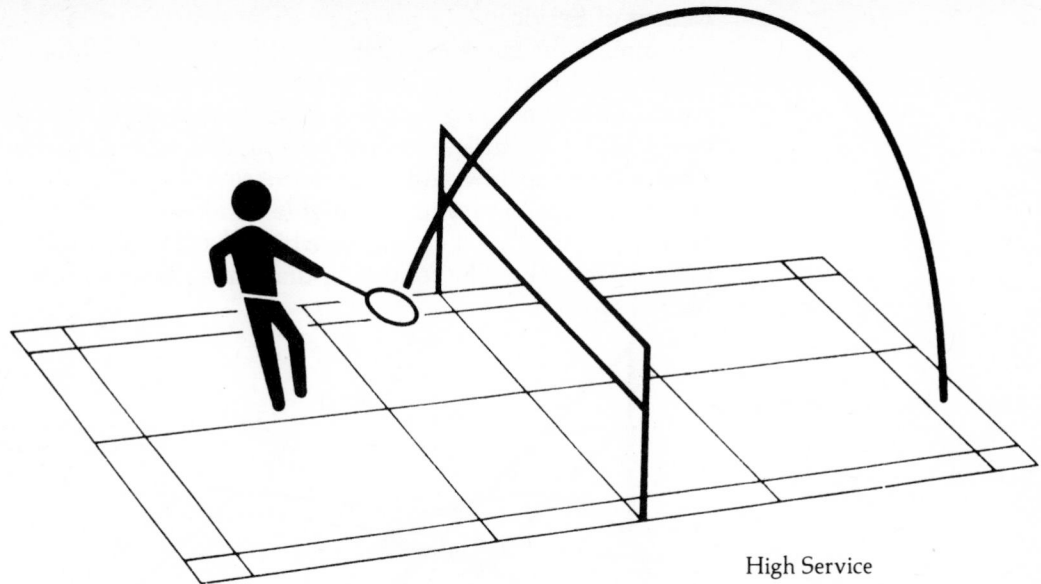

High Service

Flick Service

While the high service is used in doubles play, particularly in ladies' doubles, there is no deception in this stroke and consequently the flick service is a more popular variation to the low service.

It can be very deceptive if you can develop a low service with the wrist cocked, for just before impact you can uncock the wrist and project the shuttle to the back of the service court. Remember to look at the shuttle at the moment of impact, for many players do so on their low service but not on their flick and consequently lose any intended deception.

In performing the service you can direct the shuttle to go over your opponent's racket or it can be lowered in trajectory to a particular part of the court or directly to your opponent's body. This latter variation is commonly known as the drive service.

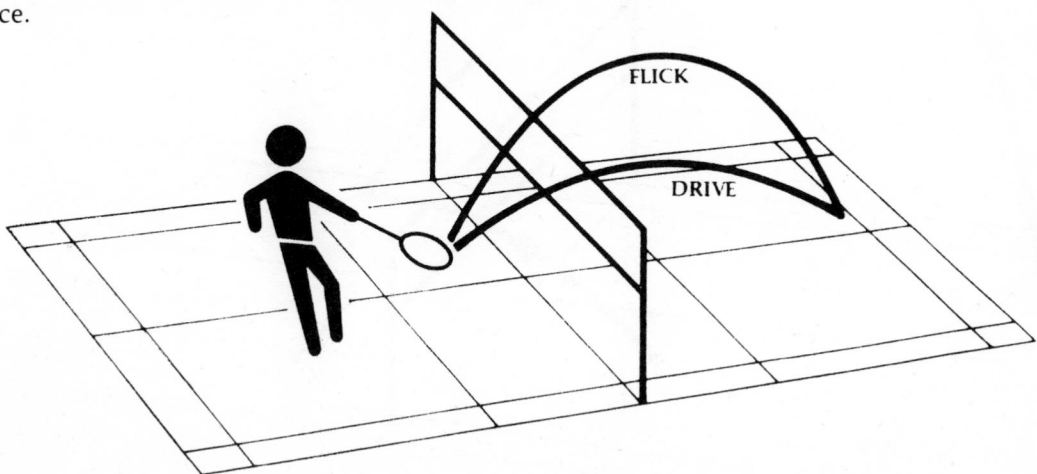

FLICK

DRIVE

Return of Service

The aim of the game is to get the shuttle onto the floor of your opponent's court at the earliest possible moment in a rally, and what better than directly off a service. Most top players make every effort to anticipate a service and knock it to the floor. This applies to low and high services alike. However, if the service is good and you are unable to attack the shuttle there are certain areas of the court to which the shuttle can be placed most effectively. The following diagrams illustrate four possible returns.

1. net return – spin net shot

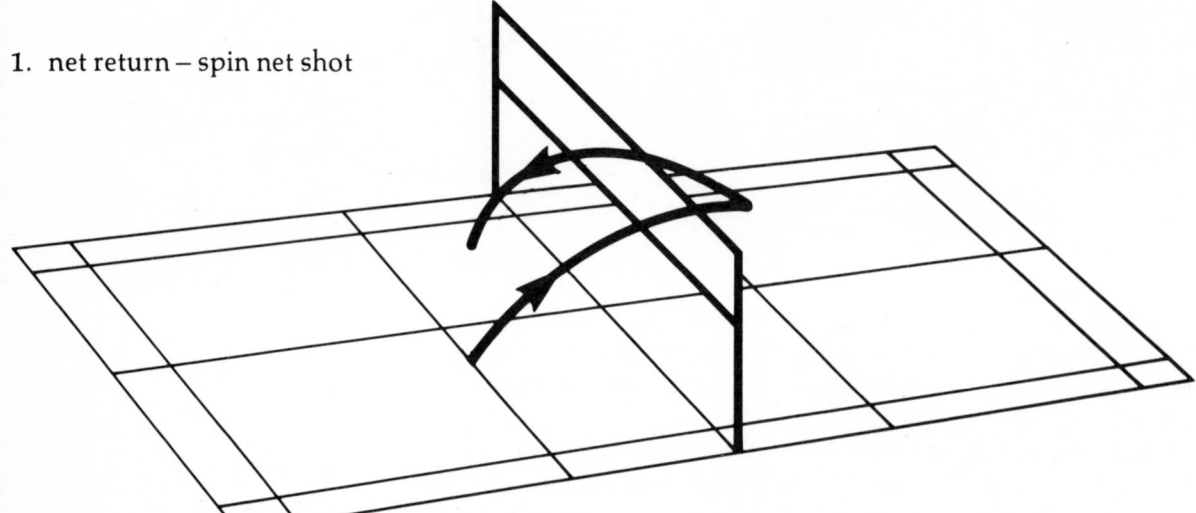

2. base-line return – underarm clear

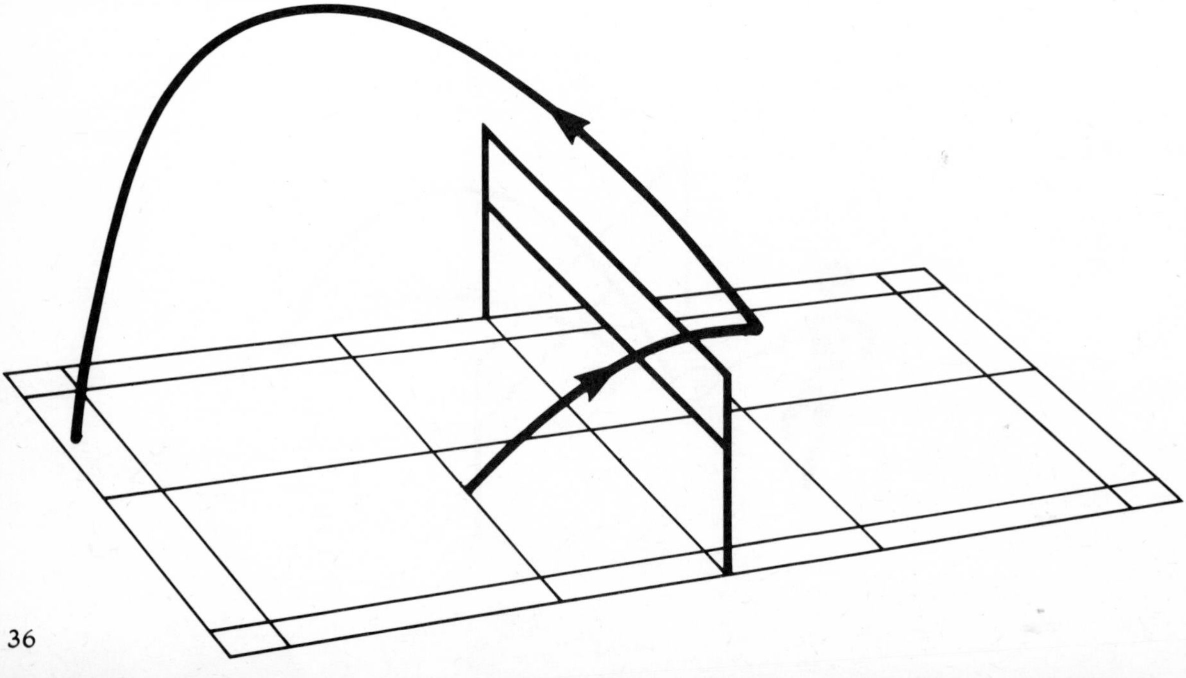

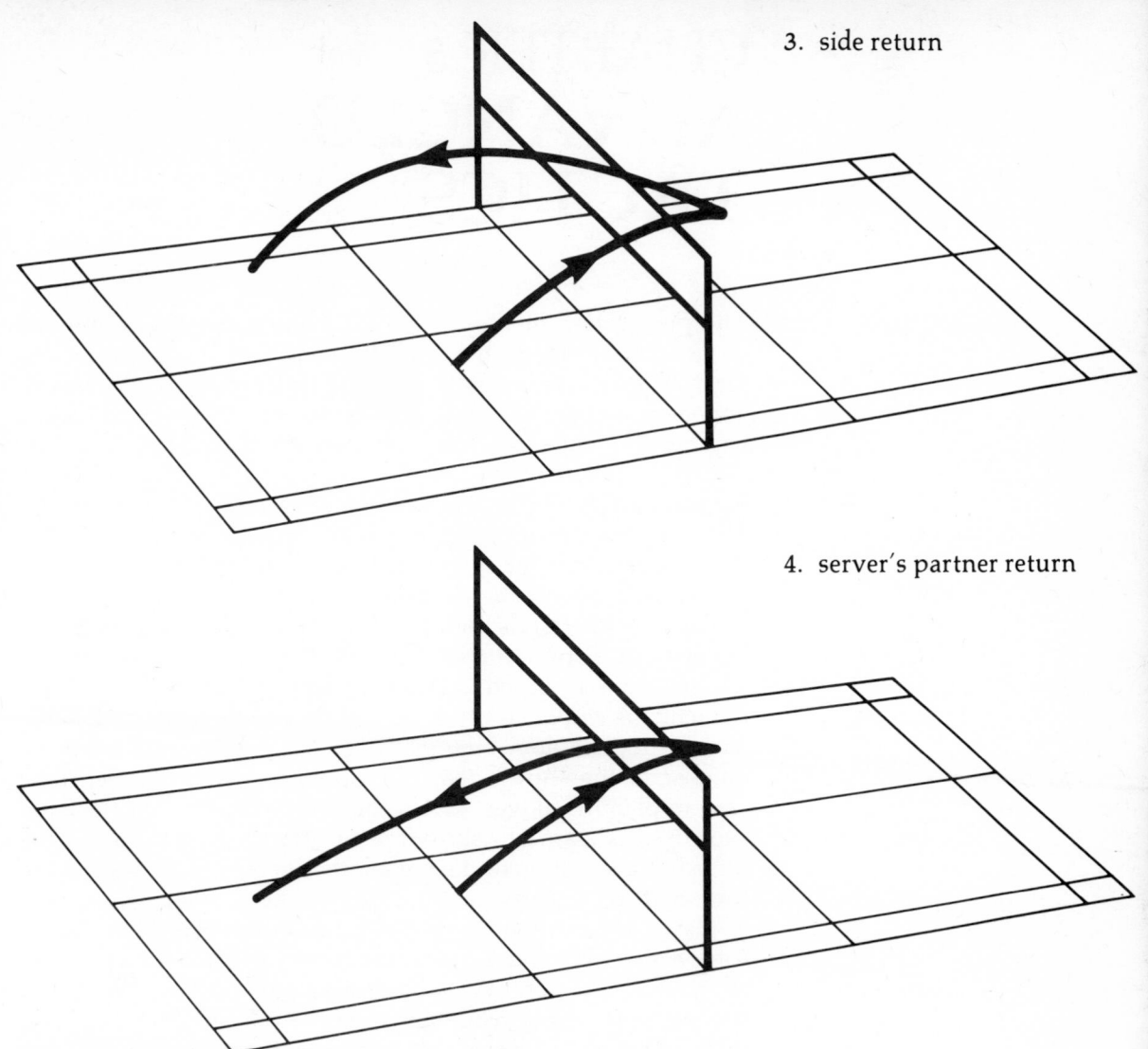

4. server's partner return

Return nos. 3 and 4 are worthy of further explanation. The side return is directed into what is commonly known as no-man's-territory, because quite often partners in a doubles combination cannot decide who should take the shot.

Return no. 4 is best achieved by brushing or slicing the shuttle. By doing this you can be more effective in disguising the actual direction of your return. It not only helps to wrong-side your opponent, but by brushing the shuttle you are less likely to hit it out of the back of the court. Brushing slows the shuttle down slightly.

One cannot stress enough in this section the importance of a good service and receipt of service. It is the basis of good doubles play. If you are not good in this department of the game then experiment and practise until you become so, or your chances of making the top are virtually nil.

CHAPTER 5
ADVANCED TACTICS

The preparation of the athlete for many sports has improved tremendously over the past decade. In badminton this improvement has brought with it a faster game, new strokes, and new tactics. We will discuss in this chapter the tactics employed by top players in both singles and doubles.

Singles Tactics

There are two main styles of play – attacking and defensive. We will consider the merits of both styles and see the advantages in being competent at both.

The attacking style seems to have the greatest success today. No one can dispute the supremacy of the top Chinese players, whose game is based on fast attacking badminton, with a tremendous emphasis on speed and fitness. So let us look at the tactics they employ. Firstly, the attack is sustained by being quicker to the shuttle than the opponent, who is given little time to plan his moves. When the shuttle is in the air the main shot used is a smash, slice drop or attacking clear, and if the return of a smash is to the net another net shot follows so as to force a lift for yet another attacking stroke. Obviously this type of play is very strenuous, and most attacking players introduce some slow clears and drops in their game to force the opponent to move whilst conserving their own energy. Sensible use of the clear prevents your opponent from moving his base forward and thus prevents him from taking drops and smashes at the earliest possible moment.

It is a common tactic to play shots to the central areas of the court. Most players develop instinctive shots from all four corners of the court, and from these positions they are able to judge distances very well. However, when forced to play from the central positions they often find it difficult to judge distances and their normal returns have to be adjusted.

When you play to the central area the possible angle of return is limited, and your opponent is thus prevented from forcing you to move excessively, and may be tempted to play a wide angle return, which often falls out of court.

Net shots placed to the centre of the net are particularly effective. These spin net shots, described on p. 28, are difficult to return to the back of the court, giving the player the opportunity to smash from a half-court position.

Liem Swie King

The smash itself is often directed to the centre of the court at the body of the opponent for the same angle-of-return reasons. Smashes vary in steepness and pace, for most players find it difficult to cope with one or other of the variations.

Liem Swie King, one of Indonesia's top singles players and All-England Championship winner, is a fine example of the attacking style.

The defensive style of singles play operates on the principle of being able to play error-free badminton and return sufficient shots from the attacking player to either force error or physically exhaust him. Of course, stroke quality, variation and deception all play a vital role if a player has sufficient natural talent, but it must be remembered that almost all shots are returnable by someone who is fast enough around the court.

A player using the defensive style will often return a smash high to the back of the court, allowing the opponent to continue his attack in an effort to force an error and tire him. Generally it is better to return the smash high, straight or to the centre of the court, rather than cross-court. A cross-court return often has the effect of opening up the court, allowing the smasher a large target area. Encouraging an attacking player to smash is a common ploy of the defensive player.

The defensive player generally plays a greater proportion than usual of high clears and slow drops so as to move his opponent from front to back and from corner to corner.

A complete player is able to play fast, attacking badminton with the flexibility to revert to defensive play at a whim. Players of such talent are few and far between but two examples stick in my mind: Morten Frost Hansen, the great Danish player, and Rudi Hartono, the Indonesian player with eight All-England titles to his credit.

Rudi Hartono – far side of the net, playing Punch Gunalan (Malaysia) in an All-England singles final.

Morten Frost Hansen

Concentrated Play

One tactic which is well worth noting is that of concentrating one's play onto a particular area of the opponent's court. For example, you can concentrate on a player's forehand by directing all returns to the forehand side of the back court. Alternatively, it may be better to concentrate on the backhand side of the back court, but it is amazing how many top class players have weaker forehands. Obviously it is necessary to play other shots from time to time and to take advantage of any openings which may appear.

The following diagram shows returns from all four corners of a player's court being directed solely to the forehand baseline of the opponent's court.

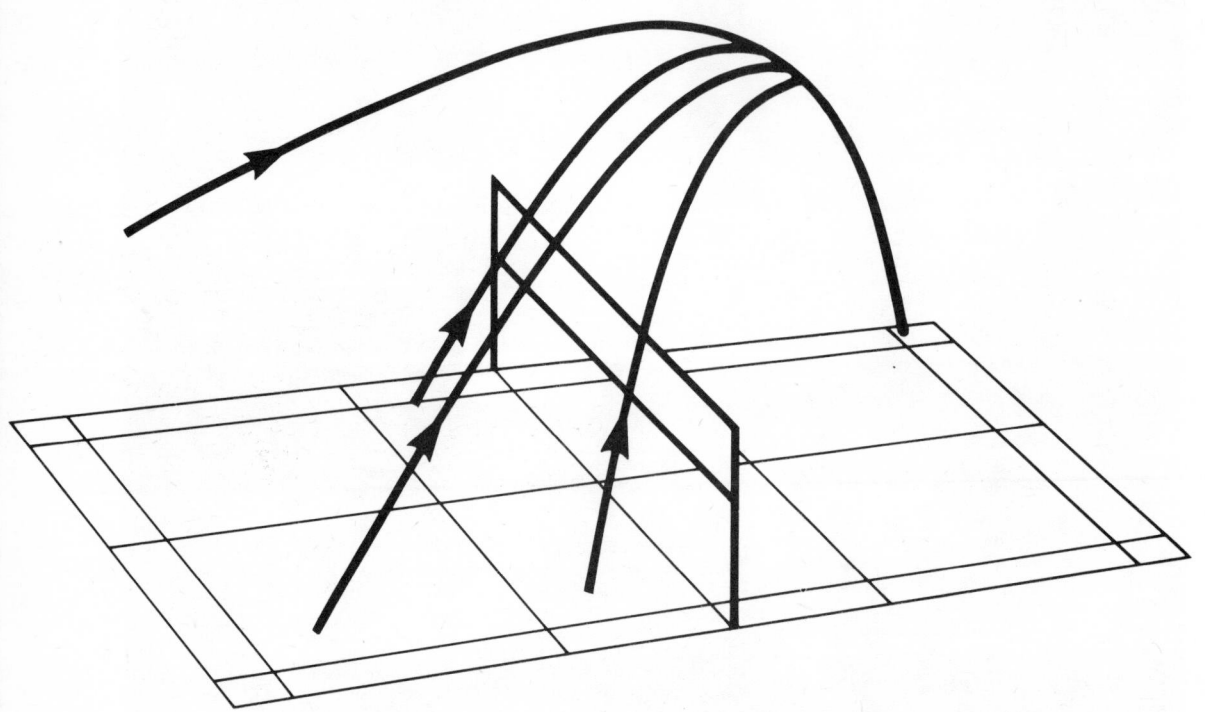

Such a ploy prevents your opponent from playing many of his best moves from other areas of the court. The forehand concentration is particularly effective against players with strong round-the-head shots.

Double Tactics
Asian Style

Top Asian pairs have been dominant in world class men's doubles competitions for a number of years. They have one major formation difference from European pairs, which we will now look at. The player who smashes from the back of the court moves forward a pace after his smash and is ready to play any shuttle which falls within a yard or so of his reach. Any other return, out of his immediate reach, whether it be to the back of the court or the front of the court, is for his partner. So if the return of the smash is another lift high over his head, his partner will step back and take it. This method has the obvious advantage of sharing the smashing load. It also allows the smasher to commit himself to a small area of the court, which is very much a danger zone for his opponents.

Most good doubles combinations have set moves where one of the pair commits himself to a likely return. This is very effective, for even if your opponent anticipates your move he is forced to avoid a particular area of the court. This often forces him to play an unnatural shot and hence increases his chances of error. Generally the smasher's partner will take up a position well behind the front service line so as to leave space for his partner to move forward after the smash if he so wishes.

Asian Style

Tjun Tjun and Wahjudi on the attack against Christian and Ade Chandra.

European Style

There are two main European styles, which are interchanged during a rally or game: the attacking or front and back formation, and the defensive or sides formation.

Obviously there are many variations as a pair changes from attack to defence during the course of a rally.

Normal Attacking (near side) and Defensive (far side) Formation.

Defensive Formation.

Derek Talbot and Elliot Stuart

Side by side formation is shown here. It is interesting to see how I am able to defend a flat smash to the body using a backhand grip on the racket.

If we compare the European style to the Asian style already discussed, we see that here the player smashing from the back of the court will normally continue to smash should his opponent return the shuttle high over his partner's head. This results in a situation where one particular player can be pinned to the back of the court by a pair with a very strong defence. Under these conditions the player is very likely to tire or make mistakes.

While on the attack the smasher's partner commits himself to the net and will usually stand close to the front service line. He does so in anticipation of a weak return from his partner's smash. There is an obvious disadvantage in a player standing in such a position and being completely out of the play against a couple strong enough to defend over his head.

So, when the two styles are compared, this is the one factor which helps the Asians to remain supreme, for it is only fair to say that in general, European pairs have a greater stroke repertoire.

One shot which is commonly used by Europeans is the half-court push. It is very much the basis of good mixed doubles, a game which is popular in Europe and little played in Asia. Consequently this shot is particularly effective against Asian players.

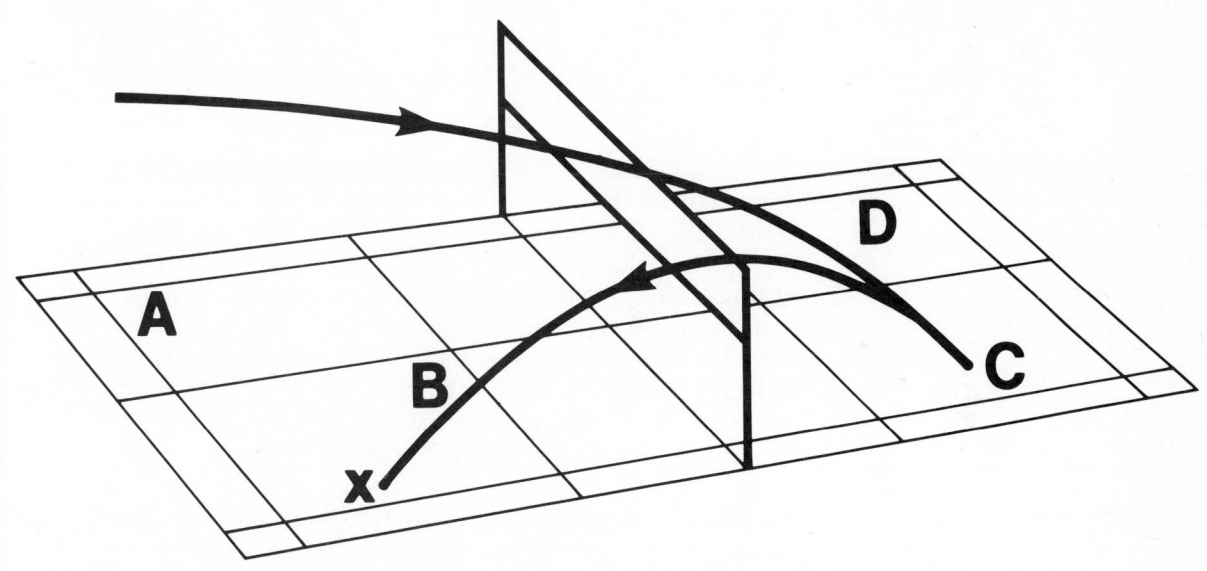

Half court push

In the attacking formation A plays a cross-court drop giving C, of the defensive formation, the opportunity to play a half-court push to the area of the court denoted by X. This shot should be placed just past B, who will move across in an attempt to play the shuttle. As a result of B's inability to reach the shuttle, A will have to move across and play the shuttle. Note the fact that both players are now in the same area of court and if the push shot is fairly flat A and B are now on the defence. Thus the attack has been turned to defence, and the push shot is one of the better shots for achieving this.

Asian players normally try to get involved in fast, flat exchanges across the net. Their doubles training methods include practising with very fast shuttles to help them become competent at this type of play (see photo on page 49).

Backhand Flat Return

Racket held well out in front of body.

Impact as far in front of body as possible, short sharp turning action of forearm and wrist.

By holding racket well in front of body one can see how it is possible to intercept a shuttle which normally would have travelled to the forehand side of the body.

Flat Returns

The racket is held well in front of the body so as to cover all possible angles. Generally the backhand grip is used, with the thumb placed up the racket handle for extra power and control. Alternatively the forehand grip can be used, pan-handle style, also covering the full spectrum of returns. It is only possible if the racket is held well out from the body. Very little arm action is involved. A strong wrist/forearm action and the pace of the oncoming shuttle produce the power.

It is a matter of personal choice whether you choose a backhand or a forehand grip for these fast, flat exchanges across the net. My best advice is for you to do whatever comes most naturally to you.

One cannot discuss doubles play without mentioning service and receipt of service because they are such a key factor. The backhand service is more common among the Eastern players and their effective use of the flick service is worthy of note.

The best style of defence appears to be as in the photograph opposite. One can see how the player is standing very square on the net. He is taking the shuttlecock very early, hitting it as far out in front of his body as possible, with a backhand grip, the grip generally used in this situation. Even shuttles directed to the forehand side can be effectively cleared in this way, using the backhand grip.

Defensive Stance

Kevin Jolly and Derek Talbot
illustrating the defensive stance at
the All-England Championships.

Mixed Doubles Tactics

This is a game which is particularly popular in the United Kingdom and in Western Europe, but sadly many other top badminton nations pay little attention to it. It is true that the demand on physical fitness makes it virtually impossible for a player to compete seriously in all three events in a tournament; consequently at least one event has to go, and in many cases it is mixed doubles. I say this is sad because I believe mixed doubles often shows a greater variation of strokes and tactics than any other event.

It is very much like chess on a badminton court, and because of this it is very difficult for this Chapter to cover all possible moves. However, I will consider some of the more important aspects.

The Role of the Girl

In general the girl will cover the front portion of the court. A good mixed player will cover the cross-court shot in a rally when her partner is playing a straight game.

One golden rule for the girl — never try and take too much. Lower level girls will try to cover the whole of the net and will, if necessary, run from side to side. Never do this! Anticipate which side the shuttle is going to and move there. If the shuttle is placed to the opposite side of the net it is your partner's responsibility to return it. Commitment of the girl is the mark of a good mixed doubles partnership and at a top level quite often the girl will commit herself to the straight reply, leaving

Christian of Indonesia demonstrating use of the forehand grip in playing a flat return.

Derek on the attack with Gillian Gilks at the net against Mike Tredgett and Nora Perry in an All-England Final.

the cross-court reply for her partner.

A good short service is also a must for a top girl.

The Role of the man

The ability to control the shuttle so that it flies low over the net from all positions on the court is an important quality for a man. One can appreciate that if the girl is, in the main, covering the net, then any shot passing loosely over the net is likely to be put away.

Shots to 'no-man's-territory' (half court just past the girl player) are particularly effective in mixed doubles. However, a good girl will step back a pace in anticipation, preventing the shot reaching 'no-man's-territory'. A good man player will tempt a girl in this way and then hit the shuttle softer or harder than she is expecting.

So the mid-court areas are of great importance and low trajectories over the net played to these areas will force your opponents to lift the shuttle, giving you the opportunity to smash.

Most points are won by a smash from either the man or, more often, the girl at the net. When on the attack, by directing your smash down the middle of the court you give your partner the best possible chance of intercepting the return.

High serving by the man to the girl is a good ploy providing your partner has an adequate defence. The tactic here is to move the girl away from her prime position at the net, thus forcing the man to cover the net. In most cases the girl is very much weaker at the back of the court than the man.

Deception plays an important role and one quite often sees the man sending the girl the wrong way at the net. On the other hand, the girl will do her best to wrong-foot the man. This aspect is covered in more detail in the next chapter.

CHAPTER 6
DECEPTION

There are many forms of deception which often involve either body movements or change of racket direction, but invariably the simpler the deception the better. It is generally the second grade of player who bases his game on complicated or fancy movements. We will look at the most important uses of deception and see just how simple they really are.

Taking The Shuttle Early

Perhaps the single most important factor in the art of deception during a rally is to move to the shuttle early before making your choice of shot. Your opponent will at all times be trying to anticipate your return and consequently the easiest way to make life difficult for him is to delay your decision on choice of shot. If you mentally commit yourself to playing a particular shot then there is a good chance that your opponent will also know your intention. However, if you move into position quickly and then decide which shot to play, the effect of your deception is much greater. If your opponent sees that your racket is within striking distance of the shuttle but he is still unsure which shot you intend to play, his best choice is to move slowly to his base position and wait until you have hit the shuttle. If he commits himself to a particular direction, you can place the shuttle in another part of the court. Over-anticipation can be a dangerous thing.

Most top players are particularly effective in their anticipation, but its effectiveness can be minimised by a player who can change the direction of the shuttle at the very last moment. Letting the shuttle drop too low before finally striking it usually limits the range of possible returns and consequently your opponent's chance of anticipation is proportionately increased. So remember: don't let the shuttle drop unnecessarily before moving your racket into the target area.

Racket Deception

Changing the direction of your stroke is a popular form of deception. You pretend to play the shuttle in one direction and then, just before impact, rotate the wrist to play it in another

Thomas Kilhström

direction. Obviously this calls for a flexible wrist, and few players could be better in this department of the game than Thomas Kilhström of Sweden.

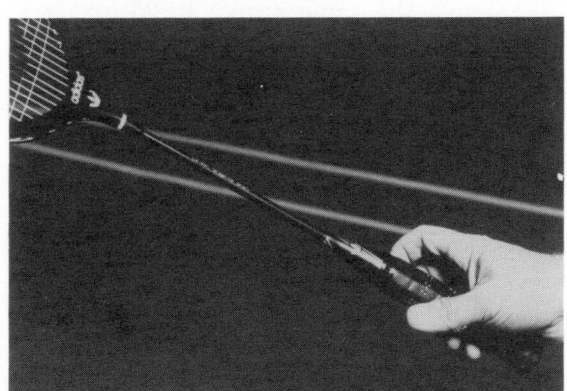

Another fine example is former All-England Champion Prakash Padukone of India.

Most players over-complicate deception of this type, when in fact it is easy to perform once one can hold the racket in one's fingers.

Prakash Padukone

Grip

Holding racket in fingers. Handle can be rotated with the fingers to cover a range of different grips. Here are two examples.

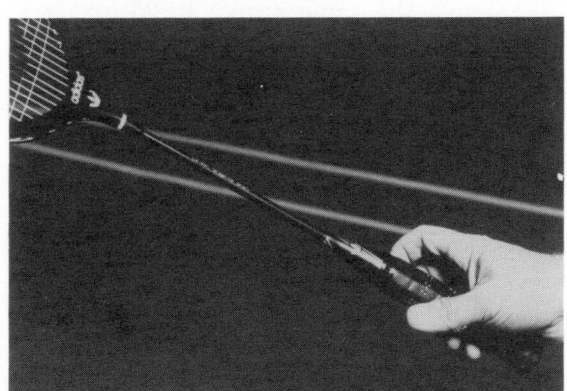
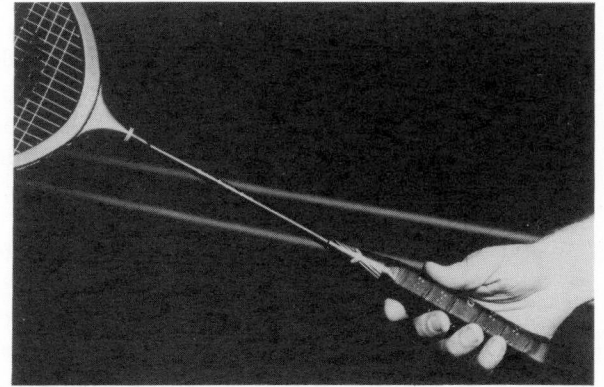

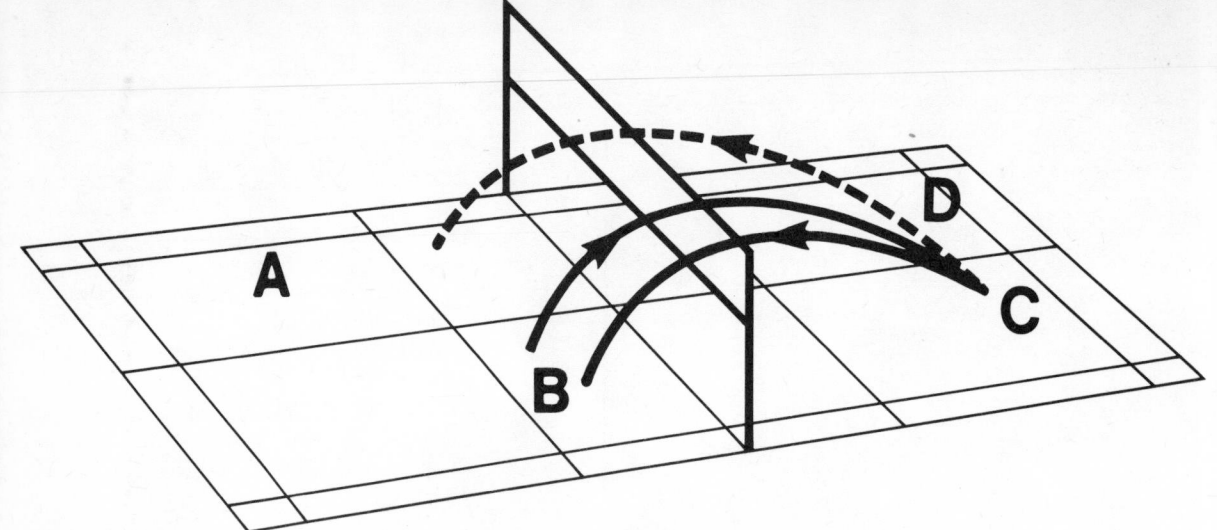

Deceptive Backhand Brush for right-handed player C.

Such a grip allows a player to roll the racket in his fingers and thereby easily change the intended direction of the stroke.

In the diagram above lady B plays a straight push to her opponent, man C, who has an open court for a cross-court reply, as indicated by the dotted line. C positions himself so as to appear to play this shot but at the last moment he rolls his wrist, brushing over the shuttle and hitting it straight. The racket action is shown in the photographs opposite.

The aim is to get the girl to move in anticipation of the cross-court reply but even if she does not, it is quite a safe shot. If you find that your girl opponent stands still on such an occasion, then the next time this situation arises play the cross-court shot. This kind of variation is an important part of deception, a factor vital to good mixed play.

Simple Deception

The most simple form of deception, and one which all players can easily develop, is to use the same technique to play a number of different strokes. For example, it is possible to clear, drop or smash with almost the same stroke build-up. It is extremely difficult for an opponent to anticipate which stroke you intend to play.

Other combinations of strokes, such as returns of drops and smashes, can be handled in the same way by developing the same stroke build-up for a net reply as for a reply to the back of the court.

Service Deception

We have already seen the importance of a good service and effective receipt of service and here, as much as anywhere, deception plays its part. Most top players are able to deliver a short service with sufficient racket control to change to a flick

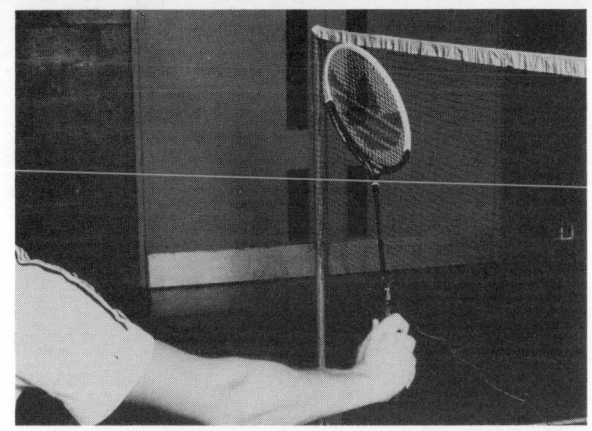

Backhand Brush

The wrist and forearm rotate in a clockwise direction. The racket head follows a curved path. The shuttle is struck well in front of the body. Placing the thumb up the back of the racket handle helps to control the brushing action.

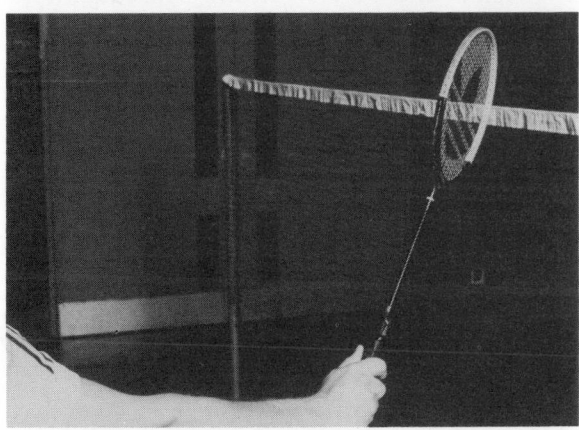
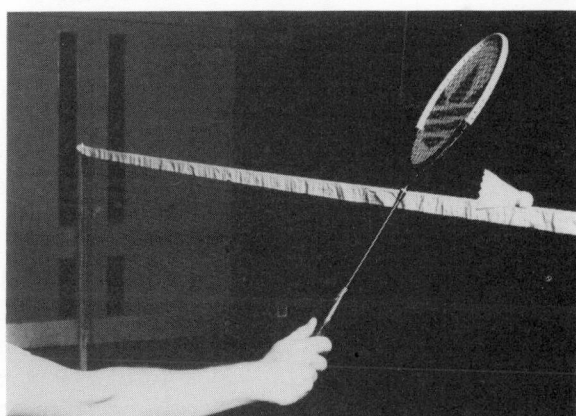

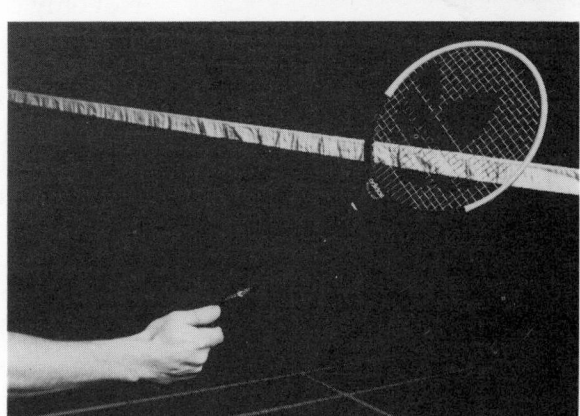

service at the very last moment. This prevents an opponent from moving early on to the service – his anticipation of your service is stifled.

A flexible wrist allows one to alter the direction of flight and this is particularly important in a low service, in order to vary the point at which the shuttle crosses the net, thus lessening the chance of an effective rush by your opponent. The same quality of wrist flexibility allows the receiver to alter the direction of his return.

Body Deception
Body movement can enhance the effect of deception but it is dangerous to either over-emphasise or over-use such movement. It is important to play more than one shot using a particular body movement or, alternatively, use different body sways for the same shot. Quite simply, either method has the effect of confusing your opponent.

It can be very effective to lean back as though to hit a clear and then at the last moment drop the shuttle. This body movement, 'leaning back', is inherent in most clears, particularly when the shuttle is well over a player's head. Consequently, a drop shot in such a situation can be very successful.

When playing a net shot, with your opponent covering the net, it often helps to sway your body in the opposite direction to your intended direction of shot. This frequently makes your opponent move the wrong way in an attempt to anticipate your shot and gives you the best chance of preventing him from attacking your net shot.

Shuttle Speed Variation
Perhaps the best example which comes to mind of a player who was particularly proficient in the art of deception is Tony Jordan – the most capped English player ever, with one hundred representations to his credit.

Not only could Tony change the direction of the shuttle at a whim, but he had another talent in being able to disguise the speed at which he hit the shuttle. Consequently, at the times when you anticipated the direction of the shot, its return was made difficult because the shuttle travelled either faster or slower than you imagined.

This type of deception is particularly effective in mixed doubles when the man and the woman in a partnership cannot decide who should play the shot.

A chapter on deception would not be complete without mentioning the legendary Finn Köbberö, the great Danish player who won the All-England Men's Doubles and Mixed Doubles titles on so many occasions. His ability to deceive has been unparalleled either before or since his playing era.

Finn Köbberö

CHAPTER 7
SPEED

In the next chapter we will look at how you can improve your movement about the court, but here we will concentrate on racket speed, and how to increase the speed of the game.

A flexible wrist and strong forearm are important in producing racket speed. Badminton is a very fast game and there is no time to play long loopy swings, as recommended in many coaching manuals. These loopy swings look nice, and indeed are fine if there is time to play them; but in most cases there isn't time, and consequently strokes produced with a short swing are most effective. Note below the position of readiness before playing a clear and the racket movement involved in producing the clear.

Racket Movement – Clear

Forehand stroke showing short racket action.

People have learned over the centuries from boxing and the martial arts the ability to deliver powerful blows over very short distances. The same principle can be applied to a racket, and a player can in fact produce very strong shots from sharp punching actions. Such actions often have a relatively slow start and a whip-like finish. This action is seen in the defensive play of some top players. Consider the photographs opposite.

The racket is out in front of the body to strike the shuttle as early as possible and to minimise the effective angle of the smash. By hitting the shuttle early one is effectively increasing

the speed of the game, by lessening the reaction time available to the opponent to play his next shot.

In the singles game, the speed can be increased by moving your base position forward. This is particularly true against a player who is not clearing high enough or hitting a good enough length of clear.

Moving your base back may be necessary against a player who plays a lot of high clears to the base line. Such clears have the effect of slowing the game down, as it is impossible for a player to move early to a shuttle which is higher than his reach and he must wait until it falls to a convenient height.

Attacking strokes such as sliced drops, flat pushes from the net, fast clears and particularly smashes are the most effective strokes to increase the speed of a game.

The ability to adjust the speed of a game is a very important factor in top-class badminton. Most players get used to playing at a particular pace both in practice and in tournaments. They feel happy at this pace and it is your job to change it. Generally, players are beaten when the opponent increases the pace of the game to a degree beyond that which they are used to. Most top players are capable of playing very fast badminton. However, it must be remembered that some players prefer to play fast,

Backhand Defence

Position of readiness with racket held well in front of body.

Follow through for backhand underarm clear.

indeed they may like it if you continually attack them. When this situation is encountered it is your task to slow the game down by playing high clears and drop shots.

Anticipation also increases the speed of a game. It is often a good idea to increase the speed at which your opponent is playing while keeping the game as slow as possible on your side of the net. Though some players play better if given very little time to think about which shot to play, generally it is desirable to have as much time as possible so as to be able to concentrate on not making an error and also to conserve valuable energy.

A top-class player who plays very much in this manner is Prakash from India, the current Commonwealth Games and former All-England Champion.

Prakash speeding up the game by intercepting a low clear to his forehand.

A stroke used to great effect in increasing the speed of a game is the flat push to the back of the court from an opponent's drop shot. Mike Tredgett is particularly effective with this shot because he has a very supple wrist, and is able to play a number of net returns as alternatives. Consider the following game situation:

Mike Tredgett playing a flat backhand push.

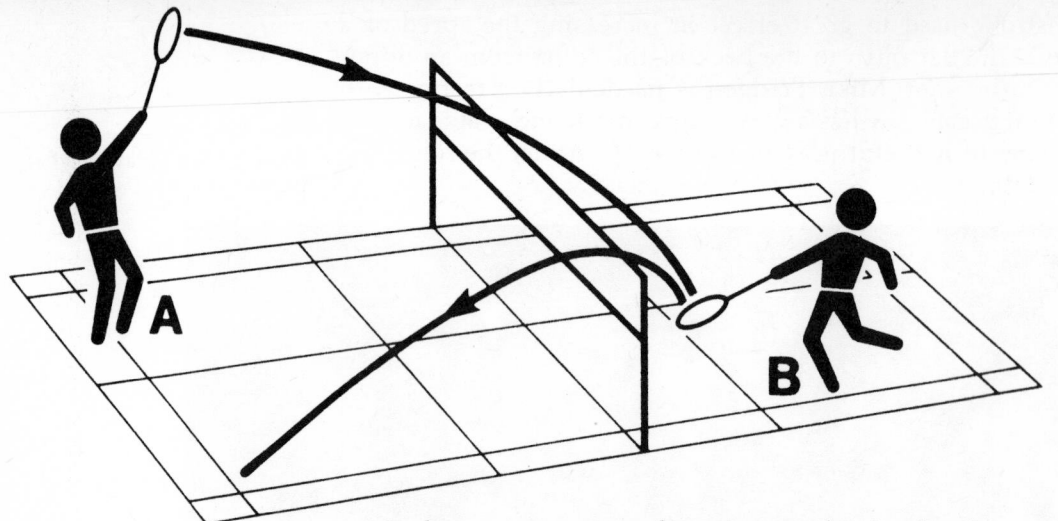

Straight Flat Push

A plays a cross-court drop, leaving his forehand court open to the flat push from B. A similar push to the back of the court can be played off a straight drop but this requires more deception and has a much higher chance of being successfully intercepted by A.

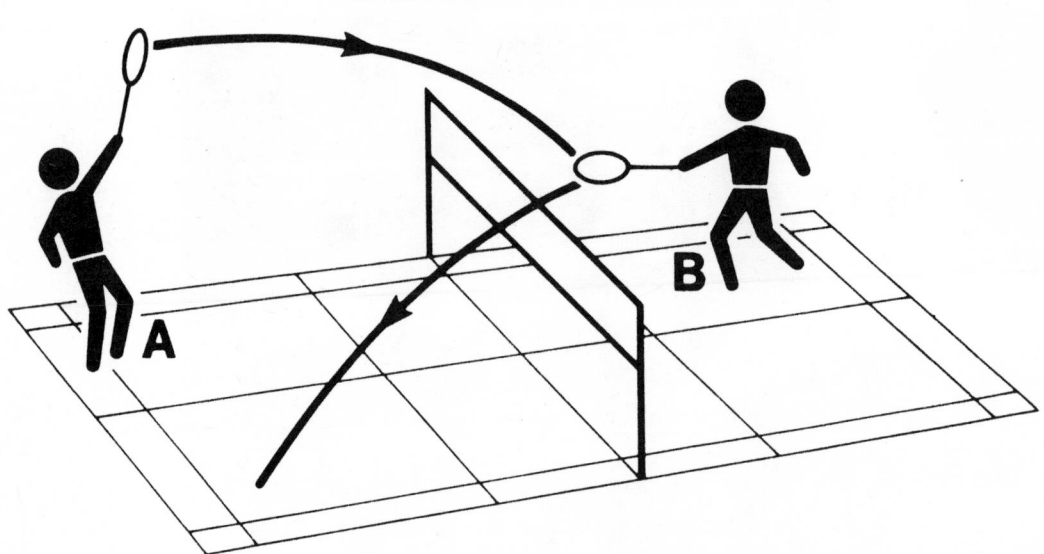

Crosscourt Flat Push

In doubles, fast flat shots to all parts of the court can be covered by partners standing side by side.

The fast flat shots increase the speed of the game and give your opponents little time to plan their moves. If you do not feel happy playing these fast flat exchanges then you must try and move your opponents from their side-by-side formation by either dropping to the centre of the net or clearing high to the back of the court.

Practising with a fast shuttlecock is a good way to improve your reflexes for this type of play.

CHAPTER 8
MOVEMENT

By now I am sure all readers will have grasped the fact that modern badminton is very fast. It is therefore more than apparent that good movement is an essential ingredient in the make-up of a champion. In singles, good movement is particularly important, for if a player is unable to sustain the pace of the game, he is unlikely to win.

It is not just a matter of moving fast, but of moving properly. Economical movement is important in a game so dependent on physical fitness. It is often necessary to preserve one's strength for moments in a game when it is most needed. In low-level clubs most players have short, jerky movements; as one progresses up the levels to international level the change to a more graceful movement can be seen.

The most important forward movement is the lunge, shown in the diagram below.

Forehand Net Shot

Backhand Net Shot

Pictures show lunging movement with shuttle being struck as close to the top of the net as possible.

From base one would normally take two long strides followed by a lunge. From this lunge position it is possible to play both net shots and underhand clears. A right-handed player can maximise his reach by lunging forward on the right leg. This applies for movements to both the right side and the left side of the net.

It is not uncommon to finish a movement with a jump, particularly backwards movements. This aids balance and with certain shots such as the smash has the advantage of enabling the player to put more weight behind the shot. In the photographs below we see the use of the jump in a smash.

Jump Smash

Saori Kondo, Japan

Showing that women also find it an advantage to jump when smashing.

Klaus Nordin, Sweden

Former European Doubles Champion demonstrates his style of jump smash.

Jump Smash

Bending the body from the hips and jumping increases the power of the smash.

It is interesting to note that many shots are played with only one leg on the ground. Many elementary books on badminton tell us to keep both feet on the ground but if one is stretching, as is often the case in a top-class match, a better balance is gained by playing the shuttle with only one leg on the ground. Consider the photograph opposite.

The player is stretching to a shot on his forehand – his balance his good.

A right-handed player will play round-the-head shots off the left leg, and backhand shots and normal forehand shots off either leg, depending on the position of the shuttle relative to the body.

Opposite are some further examples.

Forehand Drive

Playing the stroke with only one leg on the ground maximises the stretching action. Balance is still good.

Round The Head Forehand

This stroke is often performed with only the left leg on the ground. Balance is still good.

Ray Stevens, England, playing a forehand return with both feet off the ground.

Routines for Movement
Routines are an excellent method of training because they are not only good for physical fitness but also, more particularly, they help a player's movement and shuttle control. These factors all help to eliminate errors.

Routine no. 1

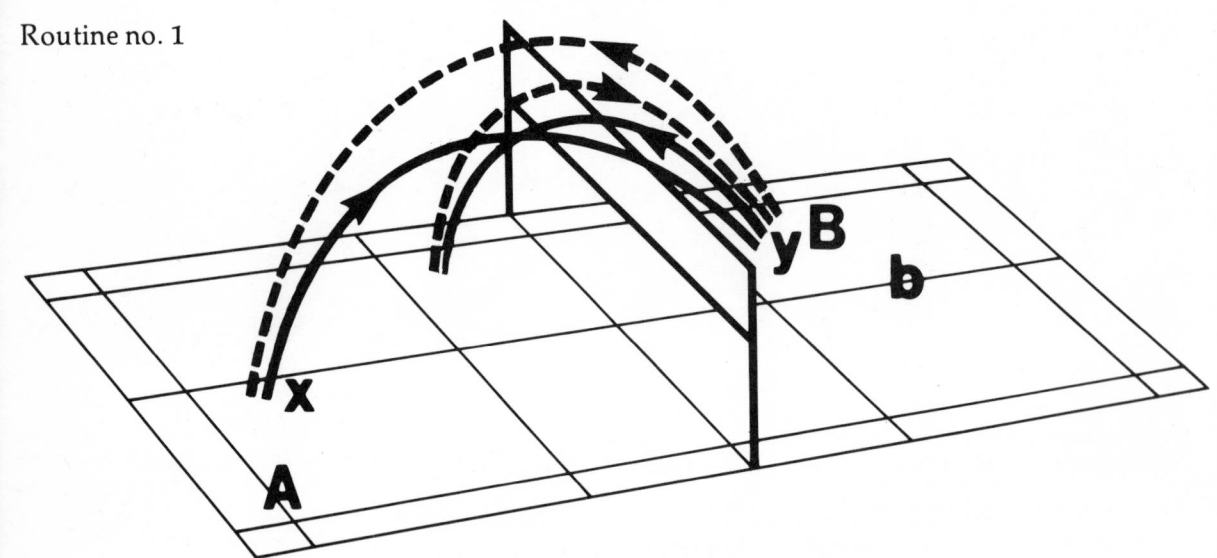

Routine no. 1
Player A plays a cross-court forehand drop, then strides to the net to play a net shot to the net return of player B, who then hits the shuttle to the base area X. The routine should be repeated twenty times without error. Player B moves from base (b) to area Y in between each cross-court drop.

Player A is thus practising cross-court movement from the base line to the net, and player B is practising movement from base to the forehand area of the net. In addition, the shuttle control of both players is improved. Once the players have accomplished the twenty repetitions without error, the same routine can be repeated with the added variation of player B being able to choose whether to play a net shot or return the shuttle to the back of the court – X. This prevents player A from 'charging' into the net after his drop shot, and the unawareness of B's return helps to improve balance.

Routine no. 2
Player A plays a round-the-head smash to player B, in area Y of the court, and player B then plays a cross-court reply to the net at area X. Player A then plays a net shot and player B returns

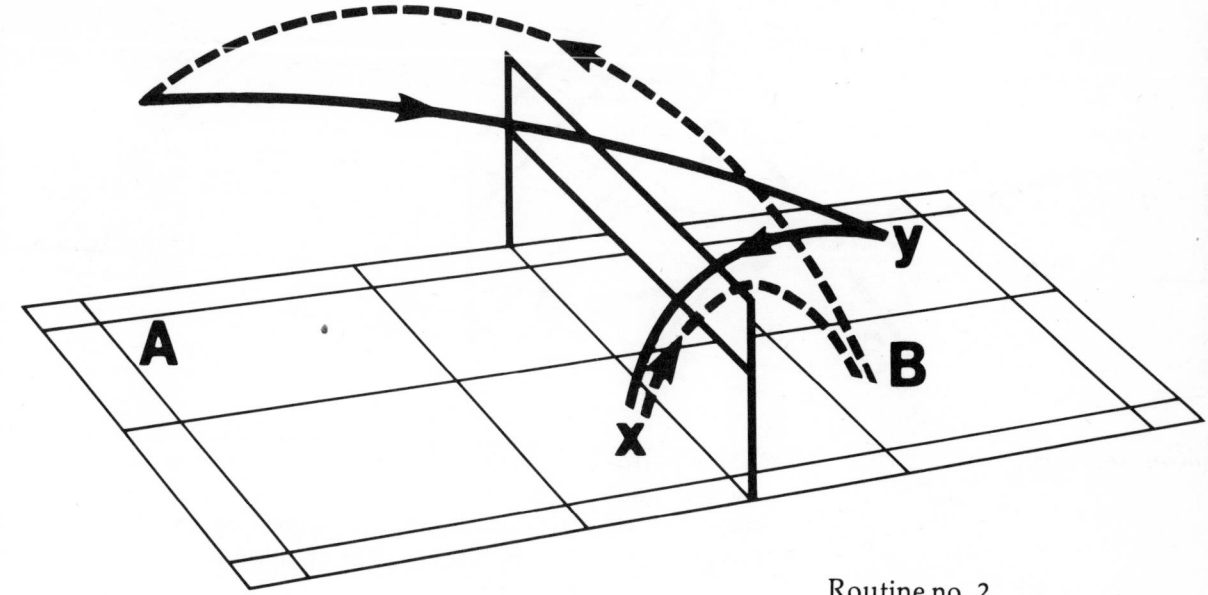

Routine no. 2

the shuttle cross court to the back of the court so that player A can play his round-the-head shot to repeat the routine. This combination of shots should be repeated twenty times without error.

Player A is able to improve his movement from the backhand far corner of the court cross court to the net and player B is able to practise movement from a half-court position on the forehand cross court to the net.

The great benefit of such routines is that players are able to practise useful combinations of shots in an actual game situation.

I am quite sure that the reader can think of many different routines of similar benefit to the two examples shown above.

Routine no. 3

This is a routine which a player can practise on his own. It is commonly known as star-runs and it involves a system of moves from base position B to all four extreme areas of the court. The player can cover movement to all four areas 1, 2, 3 and 4 in whatever order he wishes, having no set pattern, as would occur in an actual game. The effectiveness of the routine is increased if the player has someone else to shout out the numbers, one, two, three or four at random. The player must then follow this pattern of movement. It is important for the player to hold a racket during this routine and to play an

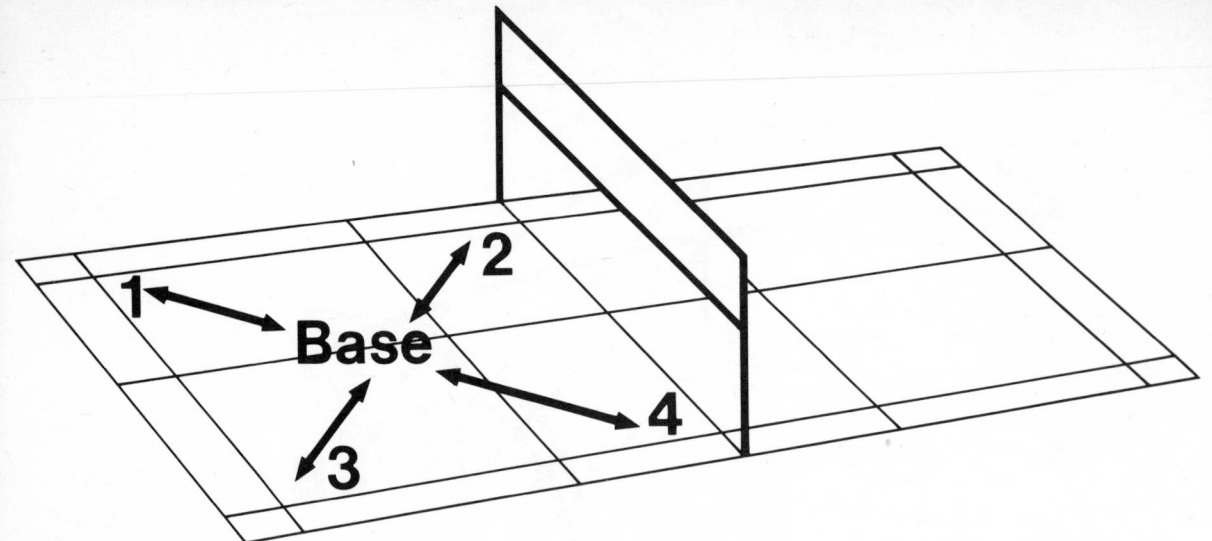

Routine no. 3

imaginary stroke at the end of each movement so as to simulate an actual game, even though no shuttlecock is used. It is normal for this routine to be sustained for five minutes although many players are capable of moving quite fast for more than fifteen minutes.

It is a good idea to practise a particular routine facing as square on to the net as possible. By limiting unnecessary turning one can save energy, be quicker to the shuttle and develop a more economical style of play.

CHAPTER 9
FITNESS TRAINING

A fitness programme should be tailored to an individual's particular weaknesses. However, there are certain areas of the body to which special attention should be paid; these areas are the legs, stomach, back, forearms and wrists. We will look at methods of developing these areas for badminton later in this chapter.

Many top-class players, particularly those from the Far East, have large legs and relatively small upper bodies and arms. Of course it is important for the arms and torso to be strong, but bulk is not necessary. The less weight the legs have to carry around, the faster they can move.

Overhead shots often involve a lot of bending backwards while forecourt shots involve bending forwards. It is for this reason that the back and stomach are so important. In the centre of the body, between the waist and the upper thighs, is the largest group of muscles in the body. If this muscle power can be released into a shot, then power is maximised. Most forms of martial art involve a turning or straightening of this part of the body to put power into blows. In badminton we can apply the same principle to some of our shots. One example is in jump smashing, where the stomach action is rather like that used in swimming butterfly stroke, in order to get extra power behind the smash.

While the arms and the shoulders are important in the production of a stroke, it is the element of timing and the turning of the forearm rather than just strength, which are the key factors. In order to produce good timing muscles need to be supple, something which will be discussed in more detail later in this chapter.

The following exercises are suggested.

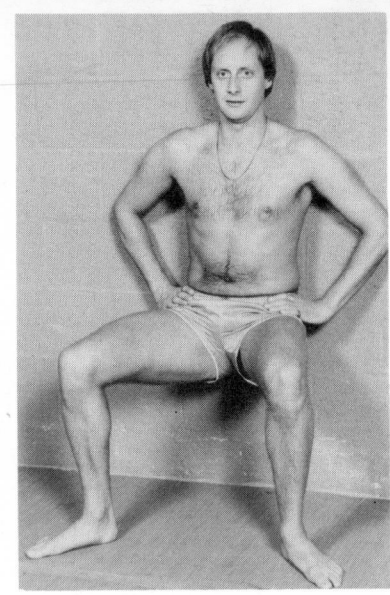

Squat Lift

Squat Stand

Legs
1. Squat Lifts
This exercise requires the use of weights and if these are not available squat standing is a good alternative. I would suggest a maximum weight equivalent to three-quarters of your body weight, and ten repetitions.

2. Squat Standing
This is a good exercise as it can be done almost anywhere and no special equipment is required. One should be able to remain in the squat position for at least three minutes.

Lunge

Calf Raises

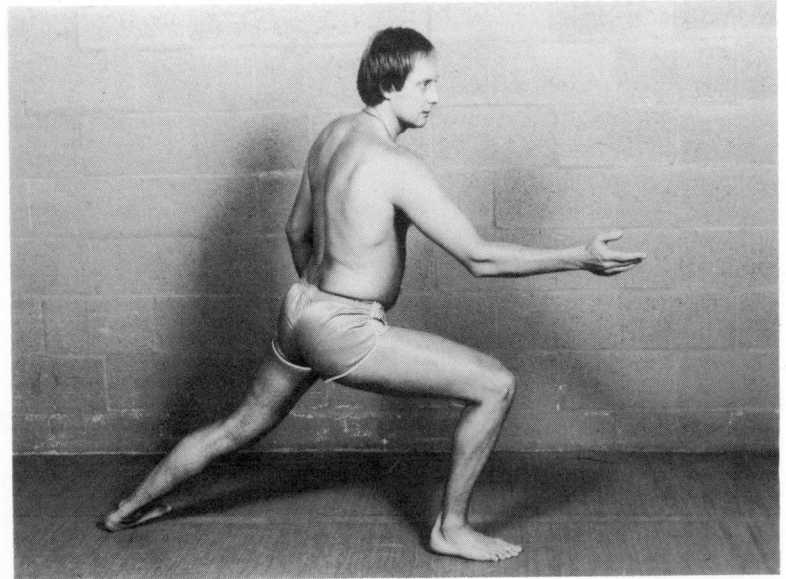
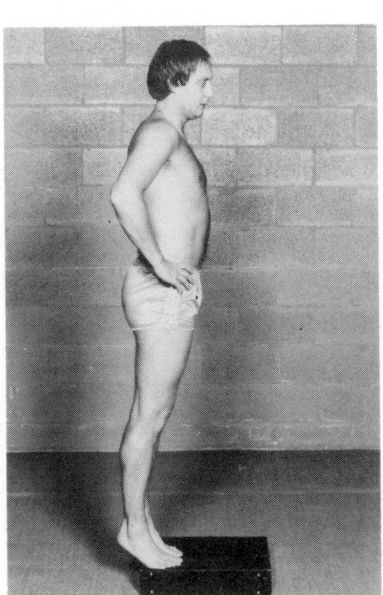

3. Stationary Lunges

It is important to do this exercise alternating the legs, even though for a right-handed player the right leg is more important for badminton. Each lunge should be held for a period of more than three minutes.

4. Calf Raises

A piece of wood or step on a stairway is perfectly adequate for this exercise. At least fifty calf raises should be done at each session.

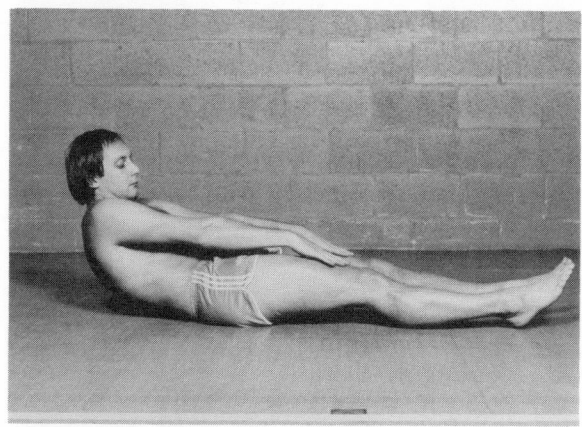
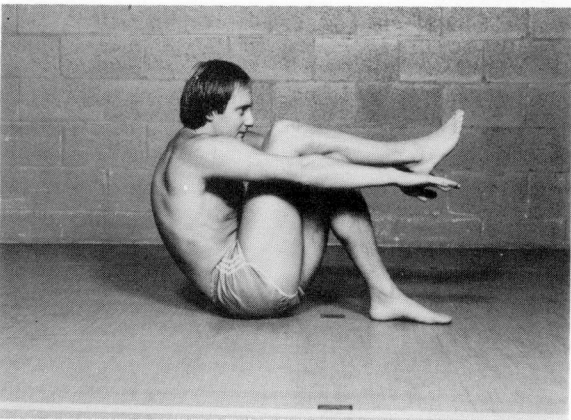

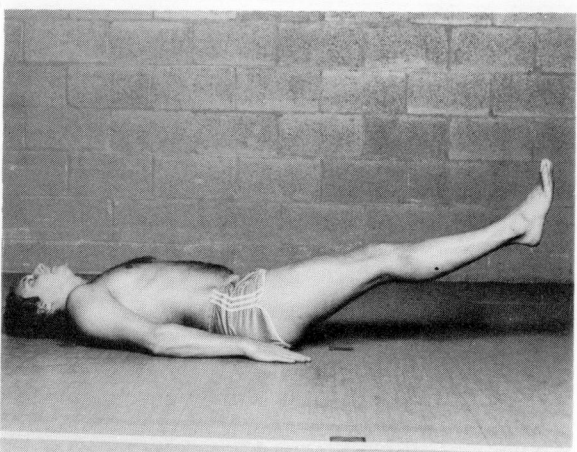

Sit ups

Stomach

Sit-ups are perhaps the best way to exercise the stomach, although there are many variations. The following are all worth doing as they exercise different groups of stomach muscles.

1. sit-up to touch knees.
2. sit-up with legs crossed.
3. sit-ups with twist.
4. leg raises.

Twenty repetitions are suggested for these four exercises.

Back

1. Arm and Leg Raises

The legs should be kept together and both legs and arms should be kept straight. Twenty repetitions.

2. Backward Crab

This position should be maintained for a maximum of thirty seconds.

Arm and Leg Raises

Backward Crab

Wrist exercise 1

Wrist exercise 2

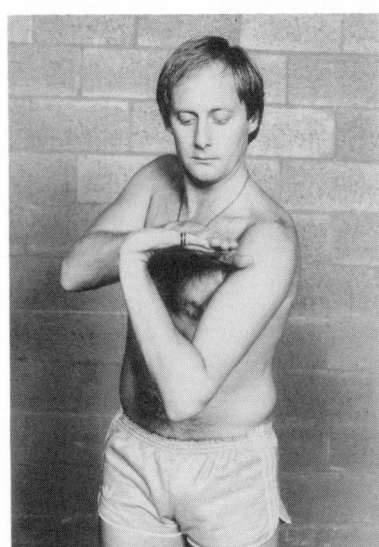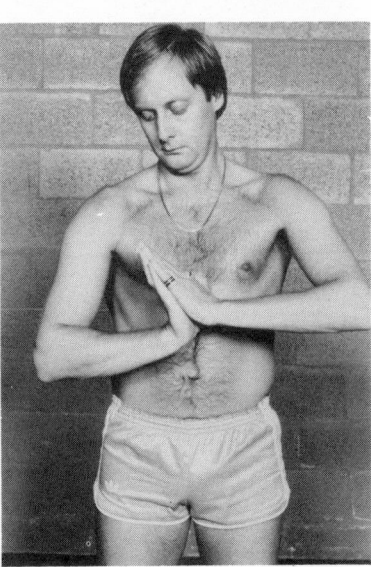

Wrists

Hold the hands in position as in the photograph above, then move both hands together first to the right and then to the left as far as they will go. Repeat ten times. Such an exercise will improve the range of movement of the wrist and strengthen it at the same time. The great advantage is that no equipment is necessary and this exercise can be done while relaxing at home or during a break at work.

Alternatively, the wrist on one hand can be held back by the other hand. This can be repeated several times, alternating hands.

Another good wrist exercise is to tie one end of a piece of string round a brick and the other round a piece of dowel; holding the dowel in both hands, wind up the string until the brick reaches the dowel. Ten rolls in each direction should be attempted.

Strength and speed

Once you have a strong body with particular tone to the areas of most importance you can concentrate on getting fit, which means working on your heart and lungs. Generally top players concentrate on strength training during the off-season and speed training during the playing season.

Strength training will involve a lot of running and weight training. Four- to five-mile runs should be done at least twice per week, and obviously the weight training involved depends greatly on the facilities available.

Speed work will normally involve shuttle runs, practice routines and suppleness training.

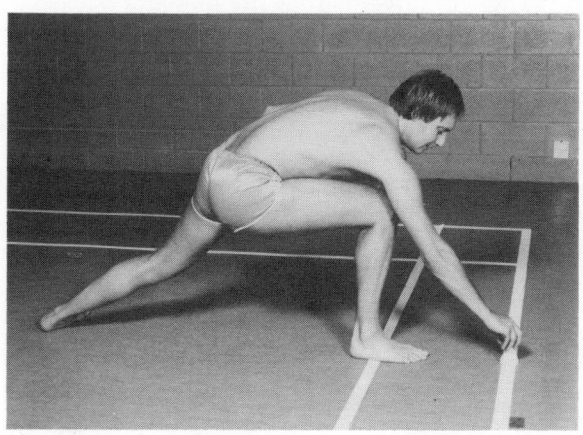 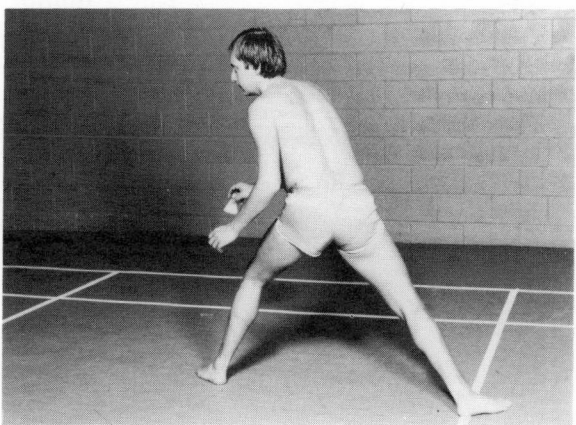

Shuttle Runs

1. Shuttle Runs

Cover the width of the court sixteen times, ensuring that you touch the extreme line on each occasion. Repeat this eight times with a forty-five second interval between each batch of sixteen runs. The whole work-out will only take approximately ten minutes.

Alternatively, it can be beneficial to vary the distances by running from the base line to the front service line, back to the base line, then to the net and back to the base line. Repeat this four times, take a forty-five-second rest, then repeat the whole procedure eight times. Ensure that when you move to the net you finish your movement with a lunge similar to that used in a game.

D

2. Practice Routines

Chapter 7 adequately covers the mechanics of these routines but it must be understood that many such routines can be very exhausting. For example, Eastern players often practise a routine called 'hundred shuttles'.

It is necessary to have two feeders and one extra person to retrieve the shuttlecocks and give them back to the feeders. Shuttles are lifted randomly to the back of the court alternately by the feeders. The player practising must smash every shuttle to a particular area of the court. Such a routine is continued for more than a hundred shuttles. In fact it is quite common for the routine to be continued for more than thirty minutes without a break.

3. Suppleness Training

The warm-up routine which I cover later in this chapter is a good system to improve suppleness. However, if there are any areas of the body which are particularly tight then concentrated exercises can be done to increase suppleness of these areas. The following are some further exercises which are particularly aimed at improving range of movement of the legs and back.

1. Sitting as shown, ensure that the knees are not bent and aim to touch your forehead on the floor in front of you.

2. Sit as shown, with the legs straight, and hold them as far apart as possible with the hands.

3. This is commonly known as the splits. You should be careful not to overstretch but, rather go down as far as possible on each occasion. Gradually, in time, you will be able to move nearer and nearer to a complete split.

Leg and back stretching

Neck Rolls

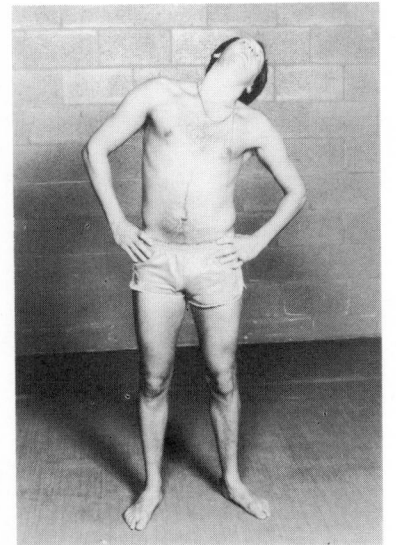

4. Taking up a position as shown, stretching to alternate legs, touching the forehead on the knee on each movement.

These stretching exercises are excellent to increase the range of movement of certain groups of muscles. If they are done regularly the muscles will become more supple. This combination of increased range and suppleness will help tremendously in improving movement and will also enable the player to get extra power into his shot.

Warm-up Routine
Most people do not realise that one can only produce full power from a relaxed condition. It is impossible to produce full power when certain muscles are tight. These tight muscles have the effect of working against those producing the stroke and consequently power is reduced.

To avoid muscle strain it is important to use a comprehensive warm-up routine before you play. The routine which I use works roughly from the head down to the feet and it comprises the following exercises:

1. Neck Rolls
Stand with your hands on your hips and roll your neck several times in a clockwise direction, then repeat in an anti-clockwise direction.

2. Arm Rotation
Rotate both arms together in a forward direction several times, then repeat in a backwards direction.

3. Forward Bends
Ensure that your knees are locked with legs straight and that

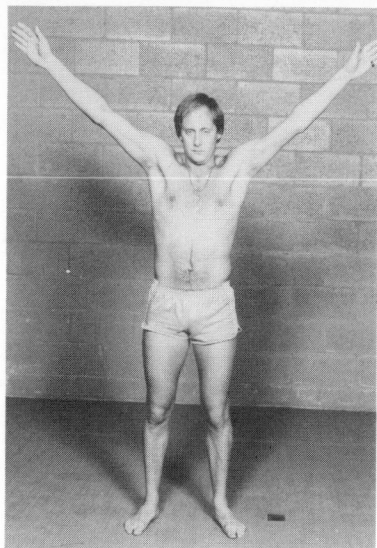

Arm Swings

Forward Bends

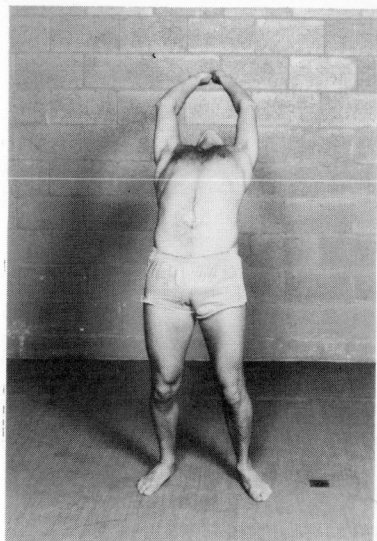

Backward Bends

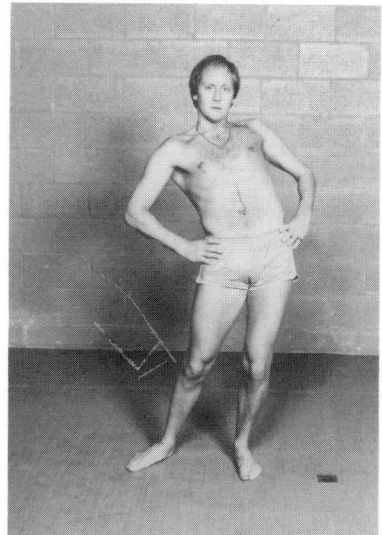

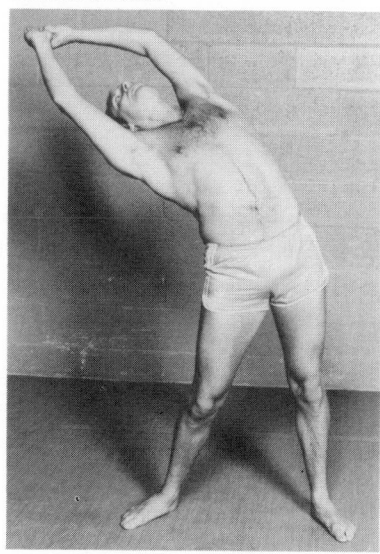

Hip Rotations
Trunk Curls
Knees Bend

your palms are pointing towards the floor. Repeat several times.

4. Backward Bends
Keep hands together and stretch backwards as far as possible. Repeat several times.

5. Hip Rotations
With the hands on the waist, rotate the hips in both directions several times.

6. Trunk Curls
With hands together and legs straight, make ten clockwise movements as shown, followed by ten anti-clockwise movements.

7. Knees Bend
Repeat several times, ensuring that the knees are fully bent.

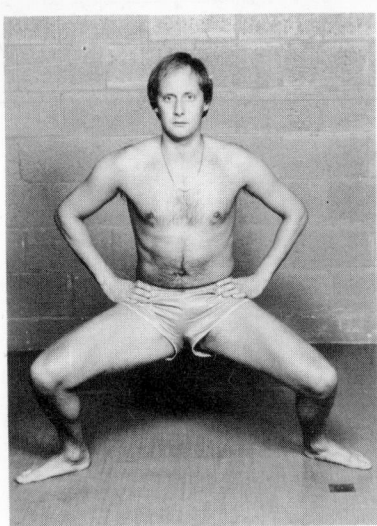

Squat Stand

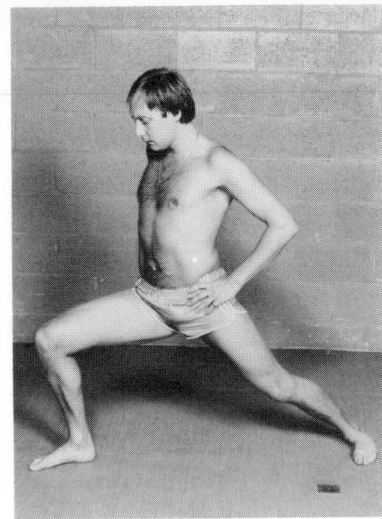

Side Squats

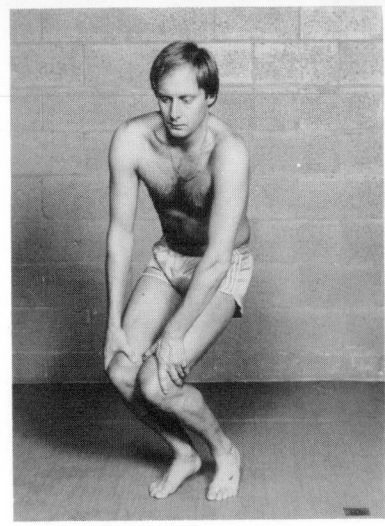

Knee Rotations

8. Squat Stand
With the legs kept as far apart as possible, hold the position as shown for several seconds. Relax and repeat five times.

9. Side Squats
Hold the position shown for about five seconds, then repeat bending the left knee. Do this five times.

10. Knee Rotation
Rotate the knees in one direction several times then repeat in the opposite direction, keeping your hands on your knees and feet together throughout.

11. Ankle Rotation
Rotate each ankle in both directions, keeping them as loose as possible to ensure maximum movement.

12. Leg Stretches
From the squat stand position sit back on one leg, keeping the other leg straight. Hold for about five seconds, then repeat with the other leg. Five repetitions on each leg are adequate.

Ankle Rotations
Leg Stretches

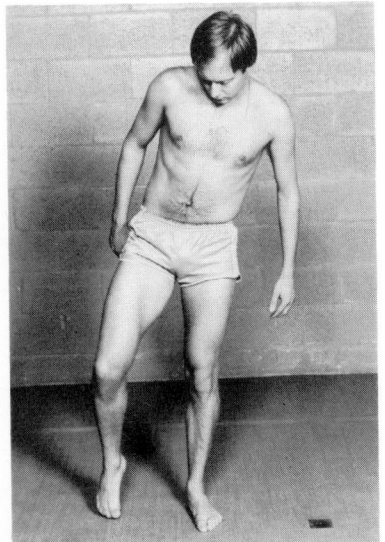

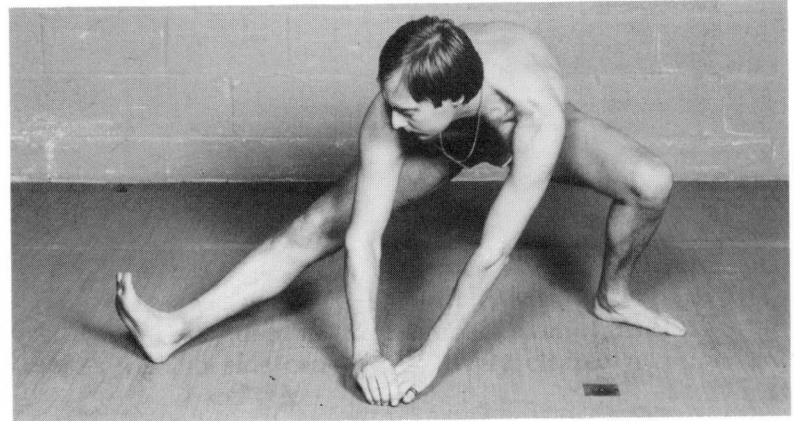

13. Hip Turns

Standing as shown, rotate around the hips first to the left and then to the right. Repeat twenty times to each side.

14. Alternate Toe Touches

Stand with feet apart. With the left hand touch the right toes, keeping both legs straight and pointing the right hand in the air. Your forehead should be on your right knee. Repeat, touching the left toes. Do the exercise twenty times to each side.

15. Bunny Hops

Complete the warm-up with three lots of ten hops, pushing the knees to the chest on each hop.

This routine takes less than ten minutes and is essential as part of pre-match preparation. In addition, a few shuttle runs can be helpful.

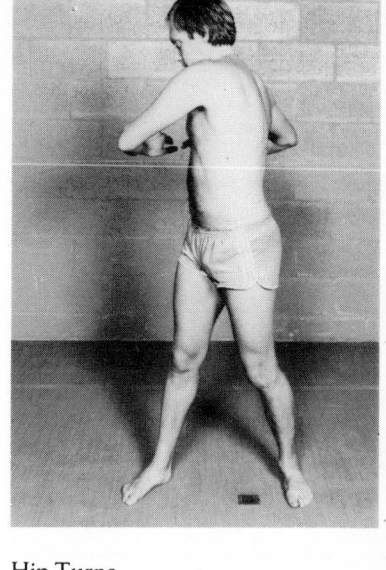

Hip Turns

Rotate around the hips first to the left and then to the right. Repeat twenty times to each side.

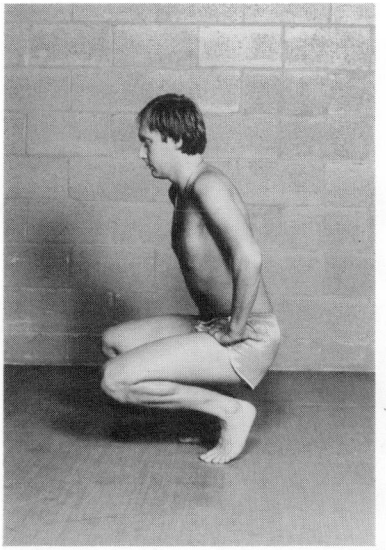

Bunny Hops

Alternate Toe Touches

With the left hand touch the right toe, keeping both legs straight and pointing the right hand in the air with your forehead on your right knee. Repeat touching the left toe. Twenty times to each toe.

Diet

A good diet is essential to peak physical fitness. One must ensure an adequate intake of proteins, carbohydrates, fresh vegetables, Vitamin C and also milk. Proteins are abundant in meat, eggs and fish, carbohydrates in potatoes, bread and rice, and Vitamin C in fresh orange juice and other fruits. Milk contains calcium and potassium important in preventing cramp.

Some players like to eat just before a match and others cannot play on a full stomach. It must be remembered that food generally takes a long time to digest, several hours in the case of meat, and therefore no benefit other than psychological can be gained by eating most foods just before a match. I personally like to eat about three hours before I play and during a long tournament I will only take food which has a fast effect, such as honey and glucose drinks. These get into the bloodstream almost immediately and are useful in providing extra energy. Carbohydrates are the best form of food for this two-to-three hour period before the match as they work relatively fast in providing energy. Slow sodium tablets are good in preventing cramp if you are going to play for several hours or in a very hot climate. But perhaps the most important piece of advice I can give is for you to drink regularly. Glucose drinks are excellent and should be taken in small quantities throughout a competition.

Certain health foods are beneficial and one particular combination which I find helpful is desiccated liver (three – six tablets), vitamin E (1 tablet) and magnesium (three tablets). The magnesium is particularly effective in increasing the supply of oxygen to the muscles.

Christian and Ade Chandra (Indonesia), taking a glucose drink during the 5 minute interval prior to the final set.

Very few players have the all-round strength of Sven Pri, the great Danish player. I understand that Sven includes cycling as a major part of his training programme. This is, of course, very good for the heart, lungs and legs. Variations in training programmes are important in preventing the player from getting bored. Sven likes cycling and other top players will find other alternatives which they can add to the basic programme of fitness training outlined above. I get my variations from practising certain Kung-Fu exercises which are particularly good for body suppleness.

Once a player has reached top fitness this does not mean that he will not 'hurt' in a tough match. A good example is a match which sticks very clearly in my mind between Sven Pri and the former Malaysian champion Tan Aik Huang at the Calgary Stampede in Canada. The contrast in styles of the two players was interesting. Sven Pri was continually smashing while Tan Aik Huang was content to defend and move Sven around all four corners of the court. The game was exciting and very strenuous for both players. Sven would not cease his attack and at setting in the third set he had pushed himself so hard that he had to leave the court to be sick on his towel. He did so on two further occasions in the third set but he would not stop smashing, and came out winner in a very close encounter. My point is that fit as he was, there were many occasions when it must have really hurt him, yet he kept going. That is a quality which is a great asset to a player, and can make the difference between defeat and success in close matches. Indeed, Sven himself has shown similar guts on several occasions in the Far East, where the extreme humidity and heat make most hard singles matches even harder.

Derek Talbot and Elliot Stuart taking advice from team manager John Havers in a Thomas Cup tie versus Sweden.

CHAPTER 10
MENTAL APPROACH

The world is made up of people, some of whom are losers and others winners. Of course everything is relative to one's environment, but for any particular environment there are people who come to the fore and others who stay in the background. It is very hard to teach a person who is basically a loser to believe sufficiently in himself to become a winner, but it is possible.

Firstly, the person must prepare in such a way as to give himself a degree of confidence. We have already covered much of such preparation – learning advanced strokes, understanding tactics, working hard on speed, movement and physical fitness. Understanding yourself and developing the ability to pinpoint weaknesses in your opponent are also important in attaining self-confidence.

If you have a strong will to win, believe sufficiently in your own abilities and give your all in your quest for success then you have the mental strength necessary to be a champion.

Of course we all admire good sportsmanship, but that does not mean you can be content to lose. Good losers as such do not make champions. In defeat you must behave in a manner fitting to your sport and in good taste with those around you – but never be content to lose against anyone. Always work out why you have lost, and how you would be able to improve your performance should you be faced with a similar match situation in the future. Then work on the areas of weakness exploited by your opponent and experiment with ways to cover your weaknesses.

By following this procedure your defeats will gradually help to improve your standard of play.

However, the name of the game is success. Do not make the mistake of being content with a victory without knowing why you won, and what you could do to win a little more easily in future. Always aim for perfection, even though common sense will tell you that it is impossible to attain.

Too many players are content with minor successes like beating someone in their local club. Of course it is good to feel pleased with such success, in fact it is essential, but always aim higher, because usually it is possible to improve that little bit more. Normally it is only the people who aim for the top who actually reach the top. Today very few players reach the top in badminton with little effort. Even the 'naturals' have to work hard, so never be afraid to give it everything you have got. It is better to try and fail than not to try at all.

So be quietly confident. Try not to show your emotions too much on court. Do not let your opponent know when he has done something to upset either you or your pattern of play.

In a series of top-class games there are many crisis stages, and it is those who can keep cool in a crisis who come out winners. Of course, it is impossible to help what is going on in your stomach; those butterflies will fly whatever you do, but looking confident and relaxed helps you feel confident and relaxed.

Interviews with a number of world champions in a number of sports have proved that the vast majority get very tense before their event. This is very important, for without this pre-match tension it is difficult to be composed during the game itself. A great number of world record-holders report that before creating their world record they felt particularly ill. This is not just coincidence, so never worry about those pre-match butterflies – they are an important part of your success.

However, composure during the event is important and just before the match starts, breathing exercises can really help. Breathing from the stomach is useful in helping blood supply to the brain and therefore very effective in taking away some of that tension. Breathe in and out slowly, keeping the stomach taut at all times and not allowing your chest to expand. In other words, you are breathing with your stomach and not your chest.

Mental approach is closely linked to tactics, for it is the mind which must decide when to speed a game up, when to slow it down, when to wipe one's brow and when to change a shuttlecock. These are all important factors and their careful use can seriously affect the outcome of a game. Unfortunately it is very difficult to teach a player such tactics, for like life itself one can only gain experience with time. However, an awareness at as early a stage as possible is very important.

Perhaps all the desired qualities can be summed up as mental strength. I can recall many situations when such strength has been vital. Perhaps if I give two examples you will understand what I mean.

In a Thomas Cup Final between Indonesia and Denmark in Bangkok a great number of Indonesian students turned up as spectators dressed in white shirts and black jackets. These people positioned themselves at either end of the court, and those at one end all took their jackets off so that there was a black background for the player of their choice and a white background for his opponent. Not only did the Danish players have to play under these unfair conditions but the crowd were shouting and jeering and on several occasions tried to rush on to the court even though it was guarded by armed police.

The other example is something that happened to me during the final round of the Commonwealth Games Team Championships against Canada in Edmonton. The match score was two–one in favour of England and I had to play the next match against Canada's John Czich, which would give England a winning three–one lead in the match if I won. Not only was it apparent that both players knew the match was vital, but the three thousand spectators also knew it and about two thousand nine hundred and ninety of them were shouting for Canada. With the temperature in the nineties the shuttles were flying fast and very difficult to control. John Czich, a very strong, hard-hitting player, was inspired at every smash and the crowd lifted him to a level far above his normal standard. I knew I must win, so was prepared to bide my time, keep cool, wait for my opportunity to forge ahead and, more particularly, for Czich to fizzle out.

To make matters worse, at match point my shoe dropped off and I had to play several shots during the rally under this handicap – a real test of concentration.

Luck was with me that day and my strong temperament helped to bring me out winner 12–15, 15–5, 15–11. The whole of the England team ran on to the court at the end of the match – all their efforts and mine had been worth it. I have never had so many hugs and kisses from so many people at once.

CHAPTER 11
UNDERSTANDING YOURSELF

Even after the most thorough preparation there are certain qualities which are hard to master, and certain areas of play are bound to remain weaker than others. Of course, different people have different weaknesses, and it is important to know your own weaknesses and develop the ability to discover and exploit those areas of weakness in your opponent.

When you are playing in a tournament, watch your likely opponent carefully in the early rounds of the competition. Not only try to discover his weaknesses, but also remember his favourite shots. Having the ability to return effectively an opponent's favourite shot can be particularly useful in destroying his confidence.

So play the game to exploit your opponent's weakness, to return his best shots and to cover your own weaknesses. If he has obviously discovered one of your weaknesses try to play in such a way as to make it difficult for him to exploit that area of court.

For example, if your weakness happens to be the forehand side of the backcourt then by playing a cross-court clear or a cross-court drop you are most likely to encourage your opponent to play the other areas of the court. By playing cross-court to his forehand you are opening out his court, leaving his backhand area open should he attempt to play another clear to your forehand.

When studying your opponent's game there are many things to look out for, but as a guide I have listed some of the more important points.

Ask yourself the following questions:

1. Is his net play good?
2. If so, does he play better net on the backhand or the forehand side?
3. Does he like to cross his net shots or play them straight?
4. Does he get height on his clears, or can they be intercepted?
5. Does he favour his backhand or is he good round the head when playing from that side of the court?
6. Can he clear from base line to base line on forehand and backhand?
7. How does he react to a concentrated clear attack to his forehand?

8. Does he retrieve easily your sliced smashes or cut drops?
9. Does he like a slow drop shot?
10. Can he defend better on the backhand side or the forehand side?
11. Does he like a steep smash or a flat smash?
12. Does he make errors off a short service?
13. Does he make errors off a flick service?
14. How does he usually play a high service?
15. How does he cope with shots played to his body?

It is amazing how many good players do not even notice whether a player is right- or left-handed. A player who is left-handed generally has a strong forehand, particularly when playing cross-court shots which seem to travel at angles very different to those from a right-hander's backhand.

Apart from these details you should also, in a hard-fought singles match, look out for mannerisms which indicate tiredness, for example shaking of the arms or legs. If you notice such tiredness, speed up the game and concentrate particularly on moving your opponent as this will make him even more tired, and thus more likely to make errors.

It is often useful to make notes on players whom you are particularly keen to beat once you have found the answers to the above questions; this will help you to remember how to play them. There are, of course, many more questions you could ask, but I wonder how many of you have ever considered your opponents even to this degree. If you do not ask yourself such questions you certainly should.

It is necessary to ask the same questions of your own game so that you are aware of your own weaknesses. This will help you cover up these areas of weakness in matches.

For example, if you have a poor backhand then do not let your opponent expose it. If possible play a round-the-head forehand shot, and when this is not possible concentrate on playing the stroke you feel most confident at – perhaps a drop. This will help considerably to reduce errors. Also, too much effort from your opponent to find your backhand may result in him hitting the shuttle out of court.

CHAPTER 12
TALBOT TIPS

I believe I have covered the most important aspects of advanced badminton, but there are certain points which I would particularly like to stress. The tips I will give you are ones which I have found to work for me. I hope they work for you too, but in any event they are certainly well worth a try.

1. Two minutes before a match do sixty seconds of stomach breathing. At the change of ends in a match a few seconds of stomach breathing helps to keep your brain alert and thinking, even though you may feel tired.

2. Always have a complete ten-minute warm-up before a match.

3. Given the choice of ends at the start of a match, always choose the worst end first. It is better to finish the match from the best side of the court and in the first game, when neither player has really acclimatised, it is less of a disadvantage to have the worst end. The quality of the ends is usually governed by the background and/or lighting.

4. Play your normal game in the first instance against an unknown opponent but if it is not successful try to play a game which is a complete opposite to the playing style of your opponent.

5. If your opponent is on a winning streak never allow him to rush you. If he tries, take your time in between rallies and if you feel you need a little time to get composure wipe your brow.

6. Plain water or glucose drink are the only things to drink during a match, and they should be limited to only a few mouthfuls.

7. If you feel you lack power in your game remember that metal rackets strung very tightly in a fine gauge synthetic gut will give you the most power. Natural gut is, of course, very good but it is impossible to achieve as high a tension with it as with synthetic gut.

8. Never play in a tournament unless you are ninety-nine per cent fit because no excuse is good enough if you lose. The most important guide for county or national selectors is the score and very rarely will they appreciate any special circumstances.

9. Finally, there is no such thing as a complete player. Remember your opponent is only human. He has weaknesses and therefore he can be beaten.

I hope that what you have read will have given you the incentive to aim for the top. If you do become a top-class player and can represent your country you will experience a wonderful way of life. All the money in the world could not buy such experiences.

However, it is not all a bed of roses for a top player, for depression and elation go hand-in-hand for him, not only because of success or failure on the court but also because of the many ups and downs in the rest of his nomadic existence. One has to accept the long delays at airports, the varying conditions of accommodation and the different customs which exist in the various countries of the world.

I can recall, in a recent trip to communist China, being treated to a sumptuous dinner at the original Peking Duck restaurant. It was a truly magnificent and memorable occasion. However, on the same tour we also had to live in an hotel at Changcha with no refrigeration, in the height of the summer. The food was far from that cooked by mum; perhaps the mosquitoes found the best food to eat. Likewise, in Malaysia I sampled luxurious first-class hotel accommodation in the centre of Kuala Lumpur and also spent one very uncomfortable night out in the country at an old army headquarters. I can vividly recall lying awake at night covered in a wet sheet to keep cool in the sweltering heat. The bed had a magnificent mosquito net which on that occasion, I am sure, held the country's mosquito population inside. To make matters worse, the sound of bats hanging from the windows and crickets croaking in the background was surpassed by the pitter-patter of rats running under my bed. The next day, covered in mosquito bites, I had to play in the finals of a local tournament.

It is only fair to say that the good experiences far outweigh the bad. When one is playing sport professionally a certain seriousness of approach is necessary, but overdoing it can be disadvantageous. To attain the highest level in a sport you must be able to relax. So my final word of advice is for you to do just that – and by doing so, enjoy one of the finest games of all time.